*The* Funding Is Out THERE!

# F*The* unding Is Out THERE!

## Access the CASH You Need
## to Impact *Your* Business

TIFFANY C. WRIGHT

NEW YORK

## *The* Funding Is Out THERE!

Access the CASH You Need to Impact *Your* Business

Published in New York, New York, by Morgan James Publishing. Morgan James and The Entrepreneurial Publisher are trademarks of Morgan James, LLC. www.MorganJamesPublishing.com

The Morgan James Speakers Group can bring authors to your live event. For more information or to book an event visit The Morgan James Speakers Group at www.TheMorganJamesSpeakersGroup.com.

This publication is designed to provide accurate and authoritative information with regard to the subject matter covered. It is sold with the understanding that neither the author nor the publisher is engaged in rendering legal, accounting, or other professional advice. If legal advice or other expert assistance is required, the services of a competent professional person should be sought.

—From a *Declaration of Principles* jointly adopted by a Committee of the American Bar Association and a Committee of Publishers and Associations.

*This book is available at quantity discounts for bulk purchases to use as premiums and sales promotions, or for use in corporate training programs.* For more information, write to Tiffany C. Wright, twright@theresourcefulceo.com

**BitLit**

**A FREE eBook edition is available with the purchase of this print book**

CLEARLY PRINT YOUR NAME IN THE BOX ABOVE

Instructions to claim your free eBook edition:
1. Download the BitLit app for Android or iOS
2. Write your name in UPPER CASE in the box
3. Use the BitLit app to submit a photo
4. Download your eBook to any device

ISBN 978-1-61448-820-0 paperback
ISBN 978-1-61448-821-7 eBook
ISBN 978-1-61448-822-4 hardcover
Library of Congress Control Number: 2013957032

**Cover Design by:**
Rachel Lopez
www.r2cdesign.com

**Interior Design by:**
Bonnie Bushman
bonnie@caboodlegraphics.com

In an effort to support local communities, raise awareness and funds, Morgan James Publishing donates a percentage of all book sales for the life of each book to Habitat for Humanity Peninsula and Greater Williamsburg.

Get involved today, visit
www.MorganJamesBuilds.com

**Habitat for Humanity**®
Peninsula and
Greater Williamsburg
Building Partner

# Contents

# Preface

**After hearing over and** over from entrepreneur after entrepreneur how hard it is to obtain capital, I decided this book was necessary. There are a number of books already available that list financing and capital sources. However, I have not seen any books that present a thorough discussion and a full description of the various sources of financing and, in particular, the when, how, and why you use them. Harnessing the collective experience of my peers – fellow small to medium business advisors and consultants – I have sought to answer these questions for small and medium businesses. The purpose of this book is to help entrepreneurs like you decide which funding source is best for your business given the type, age, and size of your business.

Before I go further I must address a critical subject: mindset. A positive mindset is critical to obtaining funding. I have met so many people – entrepreneurs, service providers and people that know them – who tell me immediately that it is nearly impossible to obtain any money for their business. And you know what? For them it is. They do not say, "I had difficulties in the past so I need help." Nor do they say, "It's been difficult," or "I've heard it's difficult," or "I have not been able to get money but I know I can somehow." No. They are completely, totally defeated. They are indeed their worst enemy. And I will now explain how.

I worked with the owner of a plumbing business that generated approximately $800,000 in revenue the previous year tell me he couldn't get a bank loan. When I told him I would help him, he told me he had tried two banks in three years and had not been able to get a loan. I asked him who he approached at the bank, a vice president or the branch manager. Did he provide an executive summary of his business or just go in and fill out an application? He grew irate. He berated me for the next 20 minutes on how difficult it is for a Black man to get a business loan. This was Atlanta in 2006. I finally conceded that the man's mind was completely made up. He absolutely could not hear me. He had decided it was too difficult and nothing I said to the contrary, including offering to help him for nearly free, could break through that barrier.

I have had people write to me about my articles on financing and say the same thing. I say, you are what you believe. If you believe your business cannot qualify for financing, it never will. You will never take the steps to obtain financing because you believe it is a total waste of your time. You will never ask for anyone's help because you do not think anyone can help you. As Napoleon Hill said in *Think and Grow Rich,* "Thoughts are things." What you think repeatedly becomes an ingrained belief. That ingrained belief, if negative, can lead to actions that sabotage you.

When you have blinders on, you cannot see. I have sat next to people who tell me how impossible it is to obtain financing. Simply impossible. As someone devoted to health and fitness, their comments are similar to those I receive from people about losing weight. In both cases, I am a wealth of information and connections. But they do not hear me. It is as if I am talking, my mouth is moving, but words are not coming out. The people totally disregard what I say. What are blinder equivalents for the ears called? That's what the people have on. They tell me what cannot be done when I am one that could truly help. It is like sitting next to a prodigious angel investor and saying no one ever invests in your business. (I have heard many tales of this too.) Once people get into complaint mode, they do not realize the damage they do to themselves.

I have helped dozens of companies obtain financing. I had to talk to owners about their business, look at the historical financials, and determine what their goals were. Some I was able to help immediately. Others required more work. Still others required creative solutions because they simply did not qualify for or appeal to more "traditional" financing sources. But every one of these existing businesses was able to obtain financing. And those that followed my recommendations were eventually able to tap into the traditional financing sources. They believed there was a way and they somehow found their way to me.

One more example. I had an owner tell me she simply could not obtain a bank line of credit. She did not know why. After analyzing her financials, I saw that her numbers seesawed. This oscillation is scary to a lender because it means the business may not have the money in a weak month to make its payment. So we had to consider actions that would help stabilize her monthly income. In addition, we looked at her customers. She had great customers. She also wanted to go after a large contract that was set aside for small businesses, but she needed a partner for to be able to fulfill the contract and needed money to deliver on the contract. In the end, we took a three-part approach. We met with a couple of bankers, both vice presidents, at two different banks that serve small businesses. They explained to her what I already knew – that banks underwrite loans based upon historical financials.

Her financials jumped from $300,000 to $1 million over a year and were rising to $2.5 million. With the one-year history she provided, the bank VPs said they could consider a $500,000 line of credit at some future time. She needed to provide quarterly statements, compiled by a CPA, at the end of each quarter for the banks to review. This would provide verifiable documentation of her increasing revenue and profit. She did get a bank line of credit for $250,000 with a quarterly review by the bank to consider increasing it as her revenues continued to increase. We also sat down with an accounts receivable (A/R) financing firm. She obtained a line of credit from this firm for $300,000. Specific receivables from high credit quality customers served as collateral for this line. She thus had $550,000 in total credit when she originally came to me with a $60,000 home equity line of credit she used for her business. Finally, we matched her with a medium-sized company in her industry niche. They agreed to partner with her on the federal contract submission and extend her a line of credit of up to $1 million if they won the contract. They did win the contract.

So no, it is not always easy to obtain financing. There may be a number of hurdles you or your business must overcome. You may have to use more expensive financing options initially, and then transition to cheaper alternatives as your business grows, becomes more profitable, and strengthens its balance sheet. There may be issues you need to address in your business to access financing. There may be issues you need to address in your financing. Often the issue is how you package your company and whom you approach. Just as your business does not appeal to all types of customers, your business will not appeal to all types of lenders. Just as your business does not appeal to every potential customer, your business will not appeal to every potential lender. Think of financing from this perspective and you will definitely meet with success.

To shift your mindset, do what you need to do. Some techniques include meditation, visualization, affirmations or prayer. See and tell yourself repeatedly that you now have all the funding or financing you need for your business. Say this to yourself throughout the day, first thing when you awaken and the last thing before you go to bed. If you have too much of a mental block regarding "financing," then focus on the success of your business. In order for your business to be successful, you must obtain the funding you need to strengthen and grow it. Visualize the success you want to have happen with your business as actually having happened. There are numerous studies in athletics, the arts and business where people visualize and then begin to feel as if what they see in their mind is definitely going to happen – it is only a matter of time. This is the feeling that will get you through, over, or around any resistance or internal obstacles to financing and success.

If you need help, there are numerous books, CDs, and videos that can help you. Search for them online, visit your local library, and order them. You can listen to them in your car, watch them on television, or on your tablet or phone. Work on you and your internal barriers if you need to. Do what you need to do to obtain financing and help drive your business to success.

If you have a negative mindset on financing, this book may help. If you read it with an open mind, your mind will begin to see the opportunities that exist and the paths to get there. If not, pass it on to someone who supports you and has a more open mind. Perhaps this will be someone you can listen to with complete confidence.

When you utilize one or more of the strategies in this book, please write me and let me know what worked for you and what your results were. Please e-mail me at twright@TheResourcefulCEO.com or twright@Cash4Impact.com.

Good luck!

Tiffany C. Wright

Atlanta

# CHAPTER 1

# The Biggest Hindrance to Business Growth

T he biggest issue most entrepreneurs say they encounter is lack of capital. Indeed, tremendous market and economic contractions occurred as a result of the excessive run-up in housing, subprime loans, and mortgage backed securities through 2007. The collapse of the housing market and the subsequent plummeting of the financial markets in early 2009 led to bank failures and severe credit restrictions. Smaller companies found it very difficult to obtain financing for their businesses during and after this period.

However, during the height of the run-up – the period from 2005 throughout 2007 – business owners often complained to me, to others, and to the media about a lack of access to capital. At that time, there was more money flowing into and out of the stock markets in the United States and Europe through brokerage firms, investment banks, hedge funds, and mutual funds than ever before.

As a business advisor who has assisted many companies in obtaining capital and as a Finance MBA who stays abreast of the capital markets – public and private, liquid and illiquid – I must say that capital is typically plentiful. For example, the U.S. still has a great number of billionaires, even adjusting for inflation and the downturn.

Yes, the downturn was definitely brutal. It resulted in hundreds of small bank failures. Yet it also enabled healthy smaller banks to expand their operations and footprint by purchasing the assets of failed banks. In the spirit of U.S. entrepreneurship and innovation, entrepreneurs in the U.S. continued to innovate and create new financial products and structures to address the Main Street funding shortages that arose. The credit restriction and economic downturn led to the birth of formalized peer-to-peer lending networks through legitimate companies. This era also birthed crowd funding sites, a brand new way to access funding, which continue to grow in use and popularity.

Therefore, ***lack of capital,*** in a broad market sense, is ***not*** the problem. The increased flow of funds into the capital markets from financial institutions, private equity ("PE") firms, hedge funds and individual investors does initially increase the size of the candidates that private equity firms target. This occurs because PE firms still only have a five to seven year time frame to spend down the larger amounts of money that they now manage. In other words, the money doubled or tripled, but the time frame in which to spend it remained unchanged.

However, the money does eventually trend its way down to smaller companies through the creation of funds-of-funds that invest in other smaller private equity firms. This comes about through employees leaving to create smaller private equity firms and through a rise in the risk tolerance of venture capital firms as PE firms or the firms they oversee buy the portfolio companies of venture capital ("VC") firms. Thus, the "trickle-down effect" continues. In addition, more small individual investors invest directly into small businesses through peer-to-peer lending networks and crowd funding sites. As these two options rise in visibility and the laws governing equity crowdfunding become clearer, more small investors will opt to invest in small businesses as a way of broadening their financial portfolios.

"What is the problem then?" you ask, if it is not lack of capital. The problem is *lack of access* to capital in a company-specific sense. Most entrepreneurs that say capital is an issue simply have no idea where to go to get it. Sometimes owners have beaten their head against the wall applying to two or three banks, only to be turned down every time. Perhaps they were persistent and spoke with five or six or seven banks. In the rare case, an owner may have scanned the classifieds section of a magazine or business newspaper in search of financing, located an ad, called the source, and then balked at the rates.

In my experience when questioned, "Where do companies go for funding?" business owners usually reply "Banks." Occasionally, they will respond "venture capitalists," especially if the inquirer specifically mentions equity financing. The average business person has either no knowledge at all of the entire range of debt that goes beyond bank financing or that knowledge is sorely limited. The same applies to the whole spectrum of equity outside of venture capitalists.

Another issue with obtaining capital is the general lack of preparedness of most companies when they go in search of capital. They want a bank line of credit, yet they do not have financial statements and may have not filed a business tax return in two years! The bank has *no* financial data it can corroborate or verify, and, therefore, has no option other than to deny the loan. Would you lend money to someone you did not know who claimed they made a certain amount of money but had no verifiable data to support the claimed earnings?

I have spoken to many entrepreneurs and the answer is an overwhelming "*No!*" However, many business owners expect a bank to say yes. Many of the companies that have approached me for help do not have any semblance of a business plan despite having revenue of $1 to $2 million. If you do not know where you are going, how do you know when you get there? The answer is, "You *don't!*"

Most of this book focuses on where to go for funding given the type of company you have and your stage of growth. However, I do want to spend some time discussing another component that also plays a dominant role in the lack of access to capital – the lack of preparedness.

For most types of financing, you will need an *Executive Summary*, which is a three- to five-page succinct synopsis of the business plan with information that is the most highly relevant to the funding source. You need an Executive Summary to give to your banker and to send to any interested potential equity investor. Writing the Executive Summary will help you understand the dynamics of your business, and understanding your own business is critical to your pursuit of funding.

If you grew to $12 million over 10 years, you must be able to succinctly explain why you will now grow to $50 million in five years. What changed? How did it change? If you are discussing your business and you do not seem to know, can you realistically expect someone else who has no familiarity whatsoever with your business to know? To pursue equity successfully, you will also need to communicate this same information in a brief PowerPoint presentation.

Another issue that contributes to a lack of preparedness is the presence of serious operational issues that hinder the successful usage of your choice of capital. If you own a service company with a debt to equity ratio of nearly 50% with few assets, your company will typically **not** qualify for additional debt, nor should it take on more. In this scenario, it has too much debt, which could lead to financial distress. Financial distress occurs when the debt service (the monthly principal and interest payments) exceeds the monthly cash flow, something that could easily occur quickly with several slow paying customers, the loss of a key customer, or a temporary or protracted business downturn. The financial distress that results from insufficient cash flow to service the debt can lead to financial failure or bankruptcy.

If you do not know your company's daily spend rate, you could be headed for financial trouble. If you cannot quickly determine how much cash you have on hand at any given time, what your breakeven point is, what your cost of goods sold is, and what your operating margin and profit margins are, you are headed for trouble. Or you may already be troubled – stressed out, continually seeking capital, and continually trying to increase revenue even though you lose money with each sale.

If your company is loaded with debt, **additional debt is not the answer**. You need an equity infusion or you need to re-structure the terms on your existing debt to more favorable terms. Or you may need to address serious operational issues. Successfully identify and resolving operating issues can increase your operating margins significantly so you can begin funding your growth out of operational cash flow (cash generated from sales).

To reiterate, in my experience, the biggest hindrance to capital is **not** lack of capital but one or a combination of the following:

1. Lack of knowledge regarding various alternative sources of capital beyond banks and VCs;
2. Lack of preparedness of the necessary documentation when approaching capital sources;
3. Pursuing debt when you or your company are already burdened; and/or
4. Experiencing operational issues that you, as the business owner, are either unaware of (inexperienced entrepreneur and manager) or ignore (in denial or too stressed to confront).

I strongly encourage you to reach out to qualified business consultants, advisors, and coaches to address issues that may be hindering your growth or keeping you up night after night.

Finally, you will achieve quicker, more lasting results in all your business efforts if you view your business as the following:

1. a marketable asset;
2. a source of long-term wealth for you and your family;

3.  a creator of jobs and an engine of the economy; and
4.  a source of investment income.

When you think of your company as an entity completely separate from you that supports the achievement of your strategic short, medium, and long-term goals, you will make near-term and long-term financing decisions that propel you forward.

 **For more articles on the subject, go to http://www.Cash4Impact.com.**

# CHAPTER 2

# Cash Flow, Capital and Business Growth

According to studies conducted by the Small Business Administration, lack of capital is one of the most often cited reasons for business failure. Another way to view capital is as a source of cash and cash flow. Businesses need cash to run operations and, if growing, to fund expansion. If your business has insufficient cash flow, it could run out of cash, resulting in business failure. Practicing cash flow management can help you identify any underlying existing or potential operational and financial issues within your business that could cause cash flow problems. I have worked with companies that have serious, operationally-driven cash management issues which cause them to need financing. Strong cash management practices can help all companies generate more cash and help stable, profitable companies reduce their need for external financing.

Profitable, stable companies whose ownership or management team manages their cash well generate sufficient capital, or cash flow, from business operations. Their cash flow statements show a positive

7

operational cash flow. Unprofitable companies typically generate a negative operational cash flow. However, fast growing companies also often generate a negative operational cash flow due to adding personnel, increasing sales and marketing costs, and incurring other expansion costs. When companies have negative operational cash flow, they need to generate cash from other activities to fund operations and expansion activities.

First and foremost, cash is king. If your business is unprofitable, it can limp along for years if it runs its operations in a way that generates cash flow, for example, if it has customers pre-pay or requires deposits. However, if its cash dries up, it has no money to pay its bills and its employees, taxes and creditors and will be forced to shut down soon after this occurs. Because of the value of cash and the need for companies of all sizes to truly understand the difference between cash, profits, and capital, I am including a hopefully illuminating discussion of the cash flow statement.

**Cash Flow**. Cash and cash equivalents – checks, wire transfers, publicly traded securities – are what your company uses to pay its bills. Cash flow is the inflow or outflow of cash at your company. Cash flows fluctuate during an accounting period – generally a month, quarter or year – and may be negative or positive at any given time. Your company's cash flow statement provides a historical record of the cash flows that occurred during the accounting period. Your company can also use a cash budget to project cash flows for future periods to identify potential shortages and plan accordingly.

Financial statements paint a detailed picture of a company's financial health. Unfortunately, most owners pay attention to the net income statement and balance sheet and ignore the cash flow statement. This happens at companies of all sizes, not just small companies. Most company accountants focus on paying bills and issuing invoices, generating historical balance sheets and income statements, reducing tax liabilities, and keeping costs low.

The treasury function oversees cash management but most companies with less than $100 to $200 million in revenue do not employ a treasurer. I have friends and acquaintances in the turnaround consulting business who can point to numerous poor cash management practices at companies of this size which led to the company's financial distress and near failure. I say all this not to scare you but to impress upon you how very important it is to manage your company's cash and detect issues and problems before or soon after they arise. This practice will help ensure you take sufficient steps IN ADVANCE to address and resolve any underlying issues and obtain capital in advance of a critical need for it.

To clearly understand your company's ability to cover expenses and liabilities, as a business owner you must regularly assess the cash flow statement. So what exactly is a *cash flow statement*? A cash flow statement records a company's cash inflows and outflows. Stated differently, this statement presents the amount of cash and cash equivalents entering and leaving your company during a specified time frame. The cash flow statement enables you as the owner, your managers, bankers and suppliers to view your company's operations from a cash perspective. Thus, all better understand how smoothly (or not) the company runs its operations, where growth funding is or will come from, and how wisely your firm spends its money. The cash flow statement breaks down the cash inflows and outflows into three sources of cash – operations, financing and investing.

***Operational (or Operating) Cash Flow.*** Operational cash flow measures cash inflows and outflows from your company's core business activities. This section of the statement shows clearly whether your company's revenue structure can cover all of its day-to-day operational expenses. If the revenues cannot, the net operating cash flow appears as a negative. If your company has a problem collecting on its receivables or is amassing unsold inventory, that issue will appear here. Late or missing payments by customers greatly restrict incoming cash. If your company has seasonal trends, cash flow may also vary by the accounting period. Monitoring the cash and projecting out operating cash flow can help you identify potential shortfalls in advance.

***Investing Cash Flow.*** Investing cash flow measures cash generated from or used in investing activities. This includes purchases or sales of equipment, property, a subsidiary or business unit. This section reflects changes in items in the asset section of the balance sheet. If your company is growing rapidly, due to all the capital expenditures made, your firm will typically show a negative investment cash flow. Struggling, asset-rich companies often show continual asset sales that offset negative or low operational cash flow. A perfect example was Kodak in 2010 through 2012, when it finally filed for bankruptcy. Kodak sold off many assets during this time period to generate enough cash to cover the huge negative cash flow its operations generated.

***Financing Cash Flow.*** When your company produces insufficient operating cash and/or experiences negative cash flow from investing, it must generate cash through financing activities. Financing cash flow measures cash generated by financing activities including the acquisition of new debt, issuance of equity, repayment of principal and issuance of dividends. This section reflects changes in the liabilities and shareholder's equity section of the balance sheet. For example, a tech company that received a venture capital investment infusion will show the proceeds here.

***Periodic Review of the Cash Flow Statement.*** In general, all other things being equal, the higher the operational cash flow, the stronger your company. By periodically reviewing the cash flow statement, rapidly growing companies can identify the need for cash in advance and utilize financing to cover the shortfalls or fund growth. A troubled company could head off financial distress by noticing negative operating cash, minimal investing cash, and significant financing cash flow. Seeing various negative cash flows on the cash flow statement could lead you to re-structure operations and revamp the financing structure before it becomes too late to do so.

An example: You examine the cash flow statement and it appears that the sole purpose of new financing your company entered into is to replace old financing. You need to dig deeper as this could be a warning sign. Your company may have brought in equity investors to pay off debt in preparation for a massive expansion. Paying off debt would reduce or eliminate cash outflows for principal and interest payments. Or your company may now have a better credit rating and have taken on new, lower cost debt to replace old debt. However, the new financing could also mean that your company is treading water and does not have the operational cash flow to pay down the debt. In this case, the new debt is simply delaying a business failure, meaning you will need to dig deep into your operational practices to determine the cause of the issues and avert business failure.

*Stability.* In general, companies with highly positive operational cash flow have high financial stability. Reviewing your company's cash flow statement on a quarterly basis can help you identify any operational cash shortages that you need to cover with financing or investing actions. Looking at all sections can tell you if your company carries too high a debt load, which could lead to financial distress, or is selling off too many assets which could leave behind a shell. A stable, growing company augments operations with cash from financing during expansion periods and takes money from operations or investing to repay financing during periods of modest or slower growth.

In the chapters that follow, I focus almost exclusively on generating cash flow from financing activities. If you read the first portion of this book and determine that access to capital may be your short-term need but operational issues or a high debt load are the primary reasons for your shortages, refer to the sections at the end of the book, including the section entitled "Resource", for assistance.

**You can also access more articles on cash flow and managing cash flow at www.Cash4Impact.com. Now on to financing.**

As companies grow, their needs change. Companies that may need one type of financing from one source at one stage of growth will benefit from another type from a different source of financing at a later growth stage. One company that fits a certain profile will be able to choose from a variety of financing sources, while another company with a different profile may only have three applicable choices. What you need and can get in the second year of your business with $200,000 in revenue and no assets will differ significantly from your business' fifth year with $2 million in revenue and $1 million in assets.

Consequently, this book will be useful to you and your company for a long time. This book will help you chart the best options for your company given your revenue range, industry and existing debt profile. It will do this for you and your business until you qualify as a bank "corporate client" – typically a company with $40-50 million in revenues and up. (Some banks qualify "corporate clients" as those with $100 million in revenue or higher.)

Companies tend to ignore building relationships with financing entities before they need them. If and when companies get around to accessing *angel* (early stage financing), VC, or PE firms, they often utilize relationships with others such as financial advisors and attorneys for introductions. Consequently, building direct relationships in advance with such funding sources, while important, is less critical. However, lack of existing relationships presents a serious obstacle for bank financing, direct lending, and similar financing.

When companies do actually build relationships with lenders, it is typically with a branch manager. What happens when the branch manager leaves? If the company was on the cusp in terms of ratios, credit score, and other criteria banks use to make lending decisions, the company will often lose its line of credit. The new branch manager will either recall or freeze the line of credit because without knowledge of the company's history, any special cases or circumstances, or the owner's character, the new manager cannot "vouch" for the company. Consequently, the new banker cannot support the predecessor's credit decision and must adhere more closely to the lending guidelines.

If you are the owner of an existing business and seek to acquire another business as a means of growing your company (in other words, you have an acquisition growth strategy), this book will provide you with a wealth of information regarding the various sources of capital to finance the purchase of that business or the assets of that business.

If you are trying to keep the amount of capital contribution you or your company must make to acquire the target company to an absolute minimum, I highly recommend *How to Buy a Business with No Money Down* by Arnold S. Goldstein. Goldstein's book has a wealth of information that will help you achieve your goal of minimum personal or business cash outlay.

# PART I

# DEBT FINANCING SOURCES

# CHAPTER 3

# Debt Financing Sources: Overview

M any stable companies with predictable, consistent cash flows prefer debt as their funding choice. Why? Because debt provides the lowest cost of capital, meaning your company pays the least when it uses debt. What does that really mean? Let me explain. When your business takes out a loan on your company's assets or against your firm's cash flows, your firm must repay the principal amount that it borrowed and the interest accrued on the loan. Your company may also have had to pay closing costs and other loan-related fees. In general, for small to medium businesses annualized interest rates – which reflect all these costs – range from 5 to 18%, depending on several factors. Therefore, your company's cost of capital equals 5 to18%.

Equity, however, does not require any principal repayments or interest payments. (Note that preferred equity may have an interest rate or specified dividend, but the payments accrue if the company has no cash to pay them. Unlike loans, nonpayment does not trigger a default.) Instead, your company must pay a proportionate share of the company's profits as dividend distributions to its equity holders. In addition, if you sell your company, you must pay a proportionate amount of the sales price to the equity holder.

For example, an investor owns 25% of your company, which generates $250,000 in profit. Your shareholder agreement states that you will distribute 40% of profits as dividends and retain the remaining 60%. You therefore distribute $100,000 in dividends – $75,000 to yourself and $25,000 to your investor. You must do this every year until you either sell the company or buy out the investor. Over a ten year period if your company is profitable, you may return well over 200% of the original investment amount to your investor, significantly more than the 5 to 18% you would have paid in interest on a loan during the same period.

Debt has other benefits. If your company is a manufacturer, equipment distributor, or other asset intensive business, carrying a high debt load on the balance sheet increases the return on assets. In addition, a high number of loans and supplier financing arrangements that you consistently pay on time builds your company's business credit.

Your company's balance sheet provides a snapshot of its financial health at a particular point in time. Debt level and type strongly impact the balance sheet. Too much debt increases your company's financial risks, but too much equity dilutes your owner's return. In addition to debt financing, your firm can use leases to acquire assets. Like debt, leases categorized as financing appear on the balance sheet as a liability.

Profitable companies with high operating cash flow have no difficulty maintaining a high debt load because they generate more than enough cash internally to make the required principal and interest payments. Companies generally make these principal and interest payments on a monthly basis.

Debt financing involves borrowing money. When you use debt financing to fund growth or operations, you take on loans or similar financing obligations. Unlike equity financing, you do not give up any ownership in your company. You pay back the principal amount you borrowed along with the interest charged on the principal amount. Debt financing often comes with stipulations – referred to as covenants or terms – about how much additional debt your company can take on, how profitable your company must remain, and the cash flow your company must generate. You can deduct the interest on debt from your company's taxable income.

Debt financing provides leverage. It enables you to stretch the funds you have in owner's equity to help accomplish company goals.

As a small business owner, your debt will typically occur in the form of loans – lines of credit, term loans or mortgages. Lines of credit and construction loans often operate as interest only loans. Some loans offer partial amortization with balloon payments at the end of the loan's term. However, most term loans and mortgages fully amortize over the period of the loan.

As your company grows into the medium-sized range, you may be able to take advantage of syndicated loans. Your company would use syndicated loans when the amount you need surpasses the lending limit of one or more banks. The banks pool their funds to provide one loan to your firm. As a medium-sized corporation, you can also tap bond financing if your firm qualifies.

The most common type of non-credit card financing for small businesses is bank loans. These include government-guaranteed loans, lines of credit. and term loans. Additional sources of debt include accounts receivable financing firms that lend against your company's receivables and equipment lenders that lend funds for equipment and use the equipment as collateral.

When you operate a business, both business risk and financial risk are concerns. In addition to driving revenue growth and profitability to achieve your goals, you must identify and mitigate both types of risk. Business risk is independent of financial risk. It is the risk embedded in your business and appears in the degree your company's operating income varies. Financial risk is tied to your company's debt level and the associated interest and principal payments.

Your business also faces financial risk from debt. Financial risk is the risk that your company will not be able to fulfill its short-term or medium-term cash needs and meet its financial obligations. Financial risk includes the increase in volatility that high interest expense causes in your company's net income. If your company has no debt, it has no financial risk because it has no interest payments or principal repayments. If your company is highly leveraged, it has a high degree of financial risk. Because financial risk first appears on the balance sheet, it is important to fully understand what a balance sheet represents.

In addition to loans, obligations your company enters into to pay suppliers and others contribute to financial risk, albeit to a lesser extent because these typically operate as unsecured debt. For example, when your company takes delivery on inventory for which it will be invoiced $60,000, its financial risk increases.

The repayment structure, interest payments, and term on your company's debt have a bigger impact than the simple presence of debt. For example, you have a 6% fixed rate, $500,000 mortgage due in quarterly installments of $10,000 over the next ten years with a balloon payment at the end. Another company has a $500,000 line of credit at an 8% variable interest rate. Assuming similar net income, your company has less financial risk because its interest rate is lower and fixed. The other company's interest rate could increase significantly over time.

Nonpayment of principal and interest payments on your company's debt can trigger a default. A debt-to-equity ratio that exceeds the maximum specified in the loan covenants can also trigger a default. When your company defaults, a secured creditor can place it into receivership. Secured creditors can foreclose upon any mortgaged property or seize the assets that served as collateral for their loans. Depending on the number of secured and unsecured creditors your company has, your business could either enter into a workout agreement with each lender or creditor or the creditors could force your company into bankruptcy or liquidation. These issues arise out of debt obligations and their associated financial risks.

# CHAPTER 4

# Banks

Ah, this is what everyone thinks of first when they think of money to grow their business. Okay, perhaps technology companies think of venture capitalists first since few nascent technology companies qualify for bank loans. Banks typically are the most risk-averse or "conservative" sources of money. They are in the business to make money, but they are also heavily regulated. Banks generate revenue by utilizing deposits to make a variety of consumer and business loans. Banks must set aside significant reserves for anticipated loan losses. This leads to a conservative mindset, but the saving grace is that this mindset enables banks to provide one of the lowest costs of capital available to small and medium businesses.

Banks sometimes get undeserved negative reviews among small business owners. However, business owners must understand which banks lend what amounts to whom and when. Some banks will not touch a loan below $1 million. Therefore, if you want a line of credit for $100,000, do not solicit those banks. Other banks will not provide a loan above $1 million. If you need a loan for $3 million with plans to expand your company's loan capacity over the next 18 months to $5 million, you should not approach those banks for a loan. Unfortunately, only a few banks explicitly state the profile of their target client or loan size. You must garner the knowledge through research, direct solicitation, and relationship building.

Banks maintain loan portfolios. If several of a bank's clients in a particular industry recently defaulted on their loans, that bank will restrict its lending to other companies in that industry. In addition, if a bank reaches a heavy weighting in a specific business category such as staffing companies, to adjust its portfolio lending the bank will often restrict or deny all loans in that category for the remainder of the fiscal year.

If you are a small business with under $10 million in revenue, a good place to start your research is with the state ranking of small business loan providers compiled by the Small Business Administration (SBA). The SBA ranks the top ten providers of SBA-guaranteed loans in each state in two categories: total volume of loans and total dollar volume. If you seek small dollar value loans (i.e., under $250,000), pursue the high loan volume group. If you seek a higher dollar value loan (i.e., $1 million and above), pursue the high dollar volume group.

If you are pursuing a bank loan and have been turned down, ask yourself some questions.

- "Did we approach someone with signature authority or did we meet with a low level employee who has to fight for every dollar above $25,000 that he or she requests?"
- "Did we dress professionally and project confidence or did we show up in shorts and appear surprised by all the questions asked of us?"
- "Did we discuss our intention to build a long-term relationship with a bank we can grow with or did we say we were shopping around for the best rates?"

- "Did we provide a loan package – an executive summary and our financial statements – or did we jot some information on a post-it note?"

If your response was the first option for each question, then read on for alternative capital sources and for what types of banks may get you to a yes. If you responded yes to the second option for each question, you must work on your packaging and preparation ***before you approach another bank or any other financing source***. If you are not prepared, cannot provide any financial statement or other finance-related information, and cannot adequately describe your business and market in words, banks and many alternative financing sources will likely continually turn you down.

A bank does not want to see a business plan. These are too long for business bankers to read. Instead, business bankers want to see a very condensed, highly relevant synopsis of the business plan referred to previously as the executive summary. This is typically three to five pages long and includes the following:

1. General overview of the business;
2. Industry overview;
3. Market overview including competitive advantage;
4. Management team including board of advisors;
5. Growth plan for the business;
6. Financing need and why; and
7. Sources and uses of funds' chart.

Each section should be approximately one to two paragraphs each. You should attach historical financials for the past three years, preferably audited or reviewed, to the Executive Summary. If the financials have not been audited or reviewed by a CPA – and the overwhelming majority of small business financials have not – then you must supply a copy of the business tax returns for the prior three years or as long as you've been in business, if under three years.

**Build and nurture a relationship with your banker.** A true business banker has decision-making authority, typically signature authority for $500,000 or above. Cultivating a relationship with a diligent, high impact banker is well worth the effort. That banker will support you when your margins drop (if kept informed), point you to other financing sources if he or she cannot directly assist and seek creative solutions if your loan needs exceed the limits for the bank. Bankers sometimes change banks so you will need to cultivate relationships with two or more bankers or follow the banker when she becomes an employee of another bank.

If your banker leaves, I strongly recommend following your banker to his or her next bank. A great banker is prized wherever she works, so your banker will operate the same no matter what institution she works for. If the banker leaves and you stay with the bank, you may no longer have anyone supporting you.

Business owners must establish relationships with their banks as soon as possible. If you anticipate needing financing in six months, go in and meet the branch manager and ask for an introduction to a vice president or assistant vice president or that bank's equivalent. Most large retail bank branch managers only have signature authority up to $50,000. If you are anything but the smallest start-up, this approval level will do little beyond providing initial working capital, which a $500,000 per year business will quickly run through. Some community bank branch managers have greater signature authority, often up to $100,000 or even $150,000. However, as previously mentioned, many bank vice presidents have signature authority up to $500,000.

"Signature authority" refers to the maximum loan amount which the person can approve on his or her own, without presenting a case to his or her superiors to get the deal approved. The more approval steps the loan must go through, the greater the likelihood the loan will be rejected. The better and closer the relationship with decision makers at the bank, the greater the likelihood the loan will be approved. For example, with sufficient signature authority, your banker can approve increases or extensions even when your company encounters short-term difficulty. Your banker believes in you as a client and acts as an internal champion for you and your company.

Companies also should not solely rely on one bank. You need to use at least two banks and build relationships at both. The first bank most small companies should pursue is their local community bank. These banks believe strongly in relationships. Sometimes their lending caps are too low for companies experiencing exponential growth (i.e., a community bank may only lend up to $6 million). However, community banks are often quite loyal and will do what they can to assist your business in procuring sufficient funding beyond their bank limits, including making introductions or referrals to other banks. Thus, these relationships are invaluable.

In addition to asking a branch manager for an introduction, as a business owner you can create these relationships by cold-calling and visiting banks of interest or by obtaining a referral. Bankers are members of the community. In smaller communities, they are often very active community members. Therefore, to meet bankers consider joining the local chamber of commerce or the Rotary Club, getting to know members of your church congregation, or taking an active role in professional, business, or non-profit organizations. Essentially, owners must network to identify and get to know the bankers.

To be prepared for bank financing, you must have proper documentation available. These include the following:

1. *Corporate tax returns* for the past three years;
2. *Personal tax returns* for the past three years. If your company has established a strong credit history and you will not

personally guarantee a loan, the bank will not request your
personal tax return;

3. *Financial statements* for the past three years, prepared by a CPA.
Reviewed by a CPA is even stronger. Audited by a CPA is the
strongest. If you have audited financials, you do not need to
provide corporate tax returns;

4. *Abbreviated business plan* or Executive Summary;

5. *Pro-forma financials* for the next three years. A pro-forma is a
nice name for projected future performance;

6. *Explanation of any negative business items* (drop in revenue, loss,
negative cash flow or similar); and

7. *Aged receivables*, especially if seeking any type of working capital
financing. Aged receivables refer to the amount of time it takes
to collect on the accounts receivables. You generate account
receivables whenever you send invoices to your customers.
Do you collect in 10 to 15 days or does it typically take 80 to
90 days for your customers to pay you once they receive the
invoice? Your aged receivables printout answers these questions.

There are many books on the market that go into detail on how to
prepare the packaging and documentation to provide to banks, how
to cultivate banking relationships, and how to build credit with banks.
Therefore, to learn more how to do just that, research those sources. For
sample executive summaries, financial statements, and aged receivable
forms, go to http://www.Cash4Impact.com/TheFundingIsOutThere/
bankchapter. No matter what financing source you pursue, a good
banking relationship is highly useful. Most of the alternative sources of
debt are to assist you when, for whatever reason, you do not qualify to
get the amount of financing you need from the bank. In other words,
most alternative sources of debt are short-term (exceptions include
equipment leasing among others), but the need for a bank is ongoing.

**SBA-guaranteed loans.** The Small Business Administration (SBA), an arm of the federal government, provides loan guarantees to designated financial institutions to encourage investment in and support of small businesses. The SBA guarantees that it will reimburse banks from 50% - 85% of the loan proceeds in the event of default, depending on the specific loan program. Banks listed as SBA-preferred lenders provide SBA-guaranteed loans.

In some states, you can get pre-qualified by an SBA loan advisor through an SBA or Small Business Development Center office. That advisor will then refer you to an appropriate bank. In other states, you must directly approach the bank for a loan. In addition, when your company does not qualify for a regular bank loan, a business banker will often refer you to the SBA program.

Due to the higher risk, SBA-guaranteed loans carry higher interest rates and high collateral requirements. The loan structure also tends to be more rigid than the terms a bank can offer with its own loan programs. However, for many start-ups or service companies with minimal collateral, SBA loans provide a viable option. SBA-guaranteed loans do have their advantages. They tend to require lower down payments, often allowing up to 90% financing of a purchase or acquisition of an asset regardless of whether the asset is another company, owner-occupied commercial real estate or equipment.

SBA loans typically offer longer terms than conventional financing, with up to 25 years for real estate financing (including purchase, refinance, and take-out of a construction loan), 10 – 15 years for machinery and equipment, and up to seven years for working capital loans. These loans are fully amortized with no balloon payments at the end, meaning the principal is fully paid off during the term of the loan.

➥*Example One: SBA loan.* A data housing firm, Acme Technologies, made the decision to spin off its data management operations in preparation for its strategic acquisition by a larger corporation. The data management division had largely gone unnoticed by the executive management team despite its successful management by the division's management. Needing to recoup some value from the division, which Acme's CFO suspected might be terminated by Acme's acquirer, Acme's CFO made the offer to sell the data management business to the division's management.

Although the division's management team was skilled in a number of functional areas including sales, operations and cash management, they had no experience handling complex financial transactions. They needed guidance so they used their network to find an advisor. They approached a U.S. Department of Commerce-sponsored Minority Business Enterprise Center (MBEC) located at a renowned university for assistance. The MBEC assigned a business advisor to help them.

The business advisor advised the management team to create a company to buy the assets of their employer. She then found a lawyer that completed their incorporation documents and successfully registered the company within three business days. Next, she spent hours requesting and compiling documentation to create an Executive Summary, pro-forma financials, and management team resumes to present to banks and direct lenders. Finally, she used her relationships with financial institutions to locate three entities that financed acquisitions and worked rapidly.

The CFO initially gave management six weeks from the time the offer was made to complete the transaction. The business advisor pushed back in conversations with the CFO and wrangled an extension. Several issues arose which the business advisor worked through quickly with the management team.

Two institutions – one direct lender and one community bank – emerged as the front runners. Both were highly responsive and flexible and recommended the use of an SBA loan. The community bank met face-to-face with the divisional management team and championed the other banking functions it could provide, along with the long-term benefits of working with them. Subsequently, the management team opted to obtain financing from the bank.

Five weeks after meeting with the business advisor, the community bank provided a Letter of Commitment (LOC) to finance the acquisition. Three weeks after obtaining the LOC, the management team closed on the financing and the purchase of the division and began operating under the new company name, Acton Technologies.

**Community Development Companies (CDCs).** Community development companies, also referred to as CDCs, provide 40% of the SBA 504 owner-occupied real estate loan program financing to entities that qualify. This is mentioned here because the 504 program is an SBA-guaranteed loan program. The CDC funds 40%, the bank provides 50% of the financing, and the business or its owner typically contributes the remaining 10%. CDCs are regional (multi-state) or community-based (county or counties or state) development organizations licensed by the SBA. To view a list of CDCs in your area, go to the SBA website at www.sba.org and search for the CDC member directory. CDCs make loans under the SBA 504 loan program to assist small businesses in acquiring or building owner-occupied real estate. The CDC processes, approves, and closes these loans. After closing, the CDC services the loan.

The SBA 504 program mandates the achievement of certain economic development requirements – typically job and income creation - through the use of its guarantees. Hence, CDCs, whose mission is tied to economic development, administer this program and lend to those businesses that help it achieve its objectives. Economic development and impact requirements vary by CDC. The CDC acts as the direct lender for the loan program and provides the funding through bond issuance.

**Community banks.** Community banks tend to be more aggressive than national banks in working with small businesses. They generally operate in one region of a state, hence the name "community" bank.

Community banks are small, nimble and generally organized to serve the needs of their communities. Some focus on consumers in the community - providing consumer banking, loans and mortgages. Others focus on business - providing loans for a number of businesses and projects.

Community banks have a much simpler structure than large conglomerate banks such as Bank of America, Wells Fargo or CitiBank. They have deposits, loans, money market accounts, and certificates of deposit. They are usually hungry to build assets. A few cater to high net worth individuals but many pursue businesses as a means of building assets. Most large corporations bank with the national conglomerates for a variety of reasons including loan capability, reach and service level. As a result, many community banks pursue small businesses and small business loans aggressively.

***When to use community banks.*** If you are a small business that primarily processes customer payments out of one location and are looking to establish or build upon a strong local presence or local relationships, community banks are for you. Find out the lending limits of the community banks in your area. The best scenario is to identify a community bank at which you can establish and build a relationship that grows as you grow. You may only need a $250,000 loan now, but in two years you may need a $2.5 million loan. If your bank's allowed loan size can grow with you, you have room to grow without needing to change banks.

To help build the relationship, place your deposits with that bank. Make sure you update your banker periodically. The more your banker knows about your business, the higher that officer's comfort level, the easier it will be for you to increase your loan size or navigate financial problems should they arise.

***Resources.*** The SBA state-by-state list of top 10 lenders to small businesses typically includes a large number of community banks. Read your community business paper – digital, online or paper – for information on SBA lenders. . Community banks that lend significantly to small businesses garner repeated attention in the business press.

**Minority-owned banks.** Minority-owned banks usually operate as a sub-segment of community banks. However, some minority-owned banks, such as Cathay Pacific, have a national reach and many more have a regional reach. These banks tend to focus on the recruitment and retention of minorities from the designated community they serve. Most of these banks focus on underserved consumers. Thus, they primarily target individual deposits, personal loans, and mortgages.

Some minority-owned banks provide a limited amount of small business loans, but they focus on small lifestyle businesses that often encounter difficulty in obtaining financing from other banks. The associated lending limits generally are low with the typical loan size varying from $10,000 to $200,000. However, several minority-owned banks focus predominantly on businesses. These tend to be regional or national chartered banks. They serve larger small to medium businesses, often providing loans in excess of $10 million.

***When to use minority-owned banks.*** Use these for the same reasons you would use the community banks. However, in this case, the "community" is based primarily on ethnicity. Note that many of these banks are located in areas in which the demographics largely match their target group, so the community can be both geographic and ethnic. These banks do not discriminate; they simply cater to their particular market segment and exhibit a heightened sensitivity to the needs of their targeted clientele.

Entrepreneurs who believe their race or ethnicity or whose focus on doing business in areas with largely ethnic demographics may have adversely affected their loan approvals in the past will often be well-served by minority-owned banks. A few examples of minority-owned banks include the following:

1. *Asian-American* owned – Summit Bank, Cathay Pacific, United Commercial Bank;
2. *African-American* owned – Citizens Trust Bank, Carver Federal Savings Bank; and
3. *Hispanic-American* owned – Americas United Bank, Sonoran Bank.

**National or Super-Regional Banks.** Some of the national banks have aggressive small business lending practices or initiatives as part of their strategic vision. These include Wells Fargo Bank, which has had a women-focused small business mandate for a number of years. Over a decade ago, Wells Fargo worked toward the goal of lending $1 billion to minority-owned companies in a 10-year period. They surpassed this goal by billions. Bank of America (B of A) is aggressive, but primarily lends small amounts to thousands of businesses. Consequently, B of A ranks highest or near highest in terms of sheer volume of small business loans disbursed, but very low in terms of dollar value per loan.

These banks host branches and other retail locations around the country. For small companies that maintain a national presence with customers in numerous states, national banks offer the breadth of reach that smaller banks cannot compete with. For small companies with international operations or customers with intentions of expanding internationally, national banks provide the credibility and currency support that smaller banks typically do not.

***When to use national banks.*** National banks and super-regional banks are the banks that everyone thinks of first; thus, my focus will be on describing alternatives to this source. If you have a good relationship with a decision maker – someone with signature authority of $500,000 or more, then speak to that person at a national bank regarding a loan. A strong relationship can trump a bank's conservative stance towards small businesses.

In addition, if you need a national presence or have overseas operations, a national bank will serve you well. Finally, many national banks offer investment banking, mutual funds, wealth management and other services. If you seek a service provider that can meet a host of your needs, then a national bank should be your first stop.

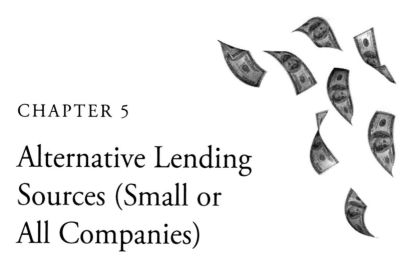

## CHAPTER 5

# Alternative Lending Sources (Small or All Companies)

G enerally, borrowing funds from alternative debt financing sources is more expensive than taking out a traditional bank loan. However, many times companies either do not qualify for a traditional bank loan or credit line or must pay very high interest rates, include a co-signer/co-borrower, and/or attach communal assets. In that case, these alternative sources serve as excellent financing sources. Remember, banks determine the interest rate charged based on risk. The highest credit grade corporate customers are charged prime. All other businesses are charged prime + a risk factor. If a bank will not provide financing, the perceived associated risk for your business is high These alternative funding sources mitigate their risks by specializing in a particular industry or asset class and compensate for this risk by charging higher fees and/or interest rates.

Below is a description of many of the different alternative sources of financing. After each description is a guideline of when your company should pursue that type of financing. These guidelines will assist in the decision process. In addition, this book lists the names of a few reputable companies in each financing category in the Resources section at the end of the book. If the listed companies do not operate or provide financing in your state, city, or town, use a search engine such as Yahoo! or Google to search the Internet for other service providers in that category or contact your local Chamber of Commerce for a list of providers.

In addition, some banks maintain lists of alternative financing providers for their clients. The banks provide this service in the hopes that, as those companies improve or mature, the firms will qualify for a bank loan and return to that bank for their loan needs. These are often banks that care about the long-term relationships with their clients. So check with your bank or other small business-friendly bank.

## Alternative Lending Sources.

**Asset-based lending.** Asset-based lending involves a business loan or line of credit secured by collateral (assets). The loan or line of credit is secured by accounts receivables, inventory, or other balance sheet assets such as machinery and equipment. Asset-based lending is also known as commercial finance or asset-based financing. Usually, manufacturers, distributors, and service companies qualify for and can benefit from asset-based financing. These are companies that generate accounts receivables and own inventory, machinery, or equipment to use as collateral. To qualify for asset-based loans or lines of credit, most commercial financing lenders need at least $150,000 in funds employed from the first day or, stated another way, a minimum credit line or loan amount of $150,000 for assets such as accounts receivables. However, many larger asset-based lenders need minimum credit lines of typically $1 million or more for loans based primarily on large equipment or inventory.

I will discuss two subcategories of asset-based financing later: accounts receivable financing in more detail in the next chapter; and factoring in more detail later in this chapter.

## Commercial finance companies or Direct lenders.

Commercial finance companies, also known as direct lenders, offer lending, leasing and other debt-like financing to small to medium enterprises, also known as SMEs. These lenders offer business and commercial loans exclusively, unlike banks which also offer consumer loans. Direct lenders secure nearly all their loans with some type of collateral. Therefore, these lenders appeal primarily to existing businesses with accumulated assets and track records.

Direct lenders typically do not have branch offices for you to visit but do have a network of associates that they work with. These lenders often have strategic relationships or partnerships with banks that subcontract or refer out loans that do not meet the bank's criteria due to loan size, borrower creditworthiness, or other factors. These lending institutions tend to be more flexible in structuring loans and can focus on building business without government interference because they are not subject to many of the rules and regulations imposed on banks.

*When to use direct lenders.* Use commercial finance companies when you do not qualify for any of the applicable regular loan programs of the banks you approach. Pursue direct lenders if you need more flexible loan terms than terms offered through traditional sources. If your company owns a large amount of equipment, real estate, accounts receivables, or other high grade assets yet has a short track record, direct lenders present a great alternative for financing your business. Those assets must be unencumbered or have low enough loan balances to justify a new or additional loan.

*Reputable sources.* CIT has ranked the highest in the nation annually for the last several years in sheer dollar volume of SBA loans provided to small businesses. CIT has a strategic partnership with Bank of America and has relationships with other banks as well.

Other reputable sources include AT&T Capital, GE Capital and UPS Capital. Many of these rank among the top 10 SBA loan producers nationally.

▶ *Example Two: Direct lending.* Julio entered into negotiations to buy a coin-operated car wash. He negotiated the seller down to 70% of the appraised value of the land plus the car wash operations at an all-in cost of $650,000. Julio then contacted Rose Ann, who works for a large national direct lender. He told her he needed a loan to purchase the car wash. In addition, he needed $100,000 in working capital to make upgrades and pay contractors.

Since the acquisition involved significant real estate holdings to use as security for the loan, Rose Ann determined that she could lend up to 85% of the appraised value of the land and building, or up to $789,000. She told Julio that she needed to show that he contributed 10% towards the total financing. Julio then approached the seller and asked him to structure the deal so that the discount Julio had negotiated was reflected as nearly 15% of the total purchase. The seller agreed, raising the price in the Purchase Agreement to $750,000 while indicating that Julio had contributed $100,000, with $650,000 more due at closing.

Julio received a $750,000 loan from the direct lender. This included $650,000 to the seller plus $100,000 to Julio's company for working capital.

Because of the deal structure, it appeared Julio had contributed $100,000 of his own money and was simply getting a refund of his money at closing to use as working capital. This is a simple example of an off balance sheet structure, which are used to finance businesses all the time. Julio enlisted a good transactional attorney to ensure he and the seller operated within their legal rights. Because the seller sold at a discount, Julio was able to obtain the loan with minimal out-of-pocket funds.

**Charge cards**. Charge cards, which require you to pay in full at the end of the 25 or 30 day billing cycle, are excellent to use for short-term, working capital financing. American Express is the best known of all charge cards. American Express requires that you pay in full within 30 days of the end of each billing cycle. The billing cycle is about 28 days.

So you may have anywhere from 30 to 60 days to pay for the product or service depending on when your company made the purchase. In addition, American Express does allow for longer payment terms for those charges related to travel and entertainment – meals, airfare and hotels, among others.

American Express reports monthly to the credit bureau. Therefore, if you are trying to build your company's credit, the American Express card is extremely useful for that purpose.

**Credit cards.** Credit cards are also best used for short-term, working capital financing of supplies and services. Due to the high fees associated with cash advances, you should not use credit cards for credit lines unless you have absolutely no other options. Credit cards allow you to delay some of your payables to better match up with your receivables, via the 30-45 day invoice and billing cycle inherent to credit cards. You can carry a balance on low-to-middle interest credit cards.

If you possess high-interest credit cards, try to transfer to lower interest cards or pursue other, longer term, lower cost financing options. Depending on the state you are based in, credit card interest rates range from 5% - 28%. (Some states cap the maximum interest rates.) The upper range is more expensive than factoring, while the middle range is comparable to accounts receivable credit line rates.

Most businesses can obtain credit card financing when the owner has decent credit and guarantees the credit card. In order to build business credit, you must obtain a credit card in the name of the business. You may have to provide a personal guarantee initially, but you should negotiate to remove the guarantee after six to 12 months. Or you may be able to open a new credit card after that credit-building period using only the business' credit, rollover the balance from the previous guaranteed card, and then close out the old card's account.

If you absolutely cannot obtain a credit card in the name of the business, then obtain a credit card in your name and use it exclusively for the business. Then have the business reimburse you for all of the expenses charged to the credit card(s). In this case, it is absolutely crucial that you maintain excellent records, lest the IRS or some other entity (e.g., a potential investor in your business) deny the legitimacy of the charges.

Some banks offer credit card interest rates similar to that of medium interest loans (7-10%). However, many charge significantly higher rates of 15-25%. Others charge low rates for purchasing products and services but charge high rates fees for cash advances.

Check with the bank you have your business checking account with first. If its rates satisfy you, use it. If not, check out other business credit card providers and their rates. An Internet search will help tremendously. For personal cards, also check with credit unions. Credit unions as non-profit entities that do not pay taxes can charge lower interest rates for many of their loans and products. However, few offer business services. Most credit unions only service individuals.

Stores such as Home Depot, Costco, and others that cater to small business owners often offer credit cards with easier qualifying terms than traditional credit cards. If you frequent a particular retail entity and either need additional credit to cover cash flow gaps or can obtain the retail cards at low interest rates, utilize that entity's credit card to make purchases there.

**When to use credit cards.** Most of you have already heard tales of people financing their businesses or ventures using credit cards so I will forego the discussion here. Credit unions excluded, nearly all banks now charge higher interest rates and a transaction fee for cash advances. Therefore, only use your credit cards for cash when absolutely necessary. Track the additional fees in your cash management system.

**Reputable sources.** Every bank issues their own or another's credit cards. A number of other financial firms also issue credit cards. First, try your bank; then try other banks. CitiBank offers company credit cards. If you are incorporated, have a business checking account and have been in business for at least several months, you have likely already received a number of solicitations for business credit cards. Review and compare these. Check sites such as Consumer Reports if you think you qualify for excellent rates and want to know what credit card providers offer them.

If you have not already done so, obtain credit cards in your business name even if you have to personally guarantee them. To help your business build credit, ensure that the credit card issuer uses your business tax ID or EIN and not your social security number.

**Factoring companies** (also called *factors*). Factoring companies pay businesses up front for their accounts receivables. Once a company has provided a service or product and invoiced the customer for the service or product, a receivable is created. The receivable is created when the invoice is **issued** to the customer, not when the invoice simply resides in the company's internal system.

Factoring companies purchase these receivables outright at a discount to the face value. Then the factor collects the payments directly from the customers when the payments are due. The discounts increase with an increase in the time it takes the customer to pay. Typically, a factoring company bases the discount on net 30, but if the factor analyzes the aged receivables and sees a usual payment history of 45 days, the factor increases the discount to account for the additional 15 days.

Factoring companies often hold back a percentage of the receivables as collateral against unpaid invoices, billings or product/service disputes. This holdback ranges from 10-20% depending on the creditworthiness of the customer. When the federal government is the customer, this holdback amount may even drop to zero.

Some factors assess pre-payment penalties in their contracts. If you pull out of the contract early, your company could owe a sizable penalty. Factoring is a short-term solution to cover cash flow gaps while you rapidly expand, build a banking relationship, or install better operational cash flow management systems. Although your company may return to factoring at different stages of its growth, you do not want to rely on factoring indefinitely. Therefore, consider signing a six-month or one-year contract. Definitely shop around for a factor that does not charge pre-payment penalties.

In addition, beware of hidden fees. Some firms require customers to pay wire transfer or administrative fees. Be sure to get the full picture up front before signing any documents. For assistance, refer to the last chapter and the Resources section.

Some factors place a cap on the credit limit or dollar value of the receivables that it will factor in any given month. Therefore, if your company intends to grow fast or anticipates a large contract or purchase order in the near future, your company should incorporate a provision for credit limit increases in the contract.

***Additional reasons to use factoring, besides pure financing requirements.*** Some companies utilize factoring firms as a credit check entity or an accounts receivable/cash management entity. Many small companies do not have the in-house personnel, expertise or process flow to quickly handle their receivables. So, instead of dealing with slow paying customers who drag out payment to 45, 60 or 90 days, companies turn the process over to a factoring firm. Essentially, they outsource their billing, receivables and cash management operations to a factor.

The companies that outsource to factors build up the other parts of their business while studying the factor's methods. As part of the outsourcing, companies obtain access to weekly or monthly accounting reports, services, and useful information on who pays when and how. When companies believe their processes are now well-scoped and efficient, they bring the receivables tracking process in-house. Still, they may utilize the factors to vet new clients or medium-sized clients for whom it is hard to obtain credit data.

Other reasons to factor include flexibility (only use it when you need it), equity preservation (grow your business to a higher valuation before bringing in equity infusion and diluting ownership), and geographic availability.

*When to use factoring.*

- When your company has contracts or purchase orders totaling $30,000 monthly (most factors prefer a minimum of $50,000) that you readily convert to receivables; Although you can find factoring firms that will handle smaller amounts, most factoring firms need the higher minimums to make the transactions profitable for their firm.
- When your company cannot obtain a bank line of credit or can only obtain one with a limit far lower than needed; and
- When you win a contract that drastically increases your monthly revenue but you do not have adequate financing to fill the orders on an ongoing basis without potentially bankrupting the company.

If you have poor internal cash management, a history of outstanding receivables, or you are signing on new customers whose creditworthiness is suspect, strongly consider using a factoring firm as an outsourced resource. In this case, your company justifies the additional cost as the factor substitutes for an employee or other service provider.

*Resources.* For more information on factoring and access to additional factoring firms, visit the International Factoring Association at www.factoring.org. Also contact the Commercial Finance Association, www.cfa.com, for information on asset-based lending including factoring.

▸ *Example Three: Factoring.* Miller Transportation, LLC, is a Georgia-based transportation broker and service provider focused on the southeast. The founder, Jay Miller, did not have good personal credit and, thus, could not secure a bank line of credit with a personal guarantee for the business. Jay also had insufficient home equity to tap into for a credit line. Jay initially bootstrapped the company with credit cards and personal savings. As a broker, the business overhead costs were minimal. (Both Jay and his one employee worked out of their respective homes)

Miller Transportation soon experienced a cash flow gap when it paid its independent operators and truck drivers within 7 to 10 days of a completed delivery but waited 30 days for customer payments. To address the problem, Jay immediately sought additional financing. Someone at an industry trade group meeting told him about factoring and recommended a firm that focused on the transportation sector. Jay contacted that firm and was subsequently approved. Since he funded nearly all of his expenses from operations, the factoring allowed him to bridge the gap between cash out and cash in.

Jay later considered accounts receivable (A/R) financing at a lower rate. However, due to the deep knowledge and relationships the factor had with Jay's customers (which pre-dated and were not specific to Jay), the factor purchased 95% to 100% of the receivables with no holdbacks. The A/R financing firm, which did not have the same industry relationships, would only finance a maximum of 80% of the receivables. Since Miller Transportation used most of its cash to fund operations and growth, the company opted to remain with the factoring firm until it had matured enough to qualify for a traditional bank loan.

Thinking ahead, Jay subsequently opened an account with a community bank and received a formal introduction to a bank vice president. The VP thought Miller Transportation would qualify for a loan after another six to nine months of the banking relationship.

**Microlenders.** Microlenders provide lower amounts of financing to those start-ups or small "lifestyle" businesses that find it difficult to obtain capital through more traditional sources due to poor credit history, lack of collateral, or lack of business history. Microlenders provide start-up funding to companies and individuals with viable ideas and businesses at higher interest rates than banks typically provide due to the higher risk profile. However, for some people, microlenders are a blessing. People with bad credit, bankruptcies, minimal assets or little advanced schooling all potentially qualify for micro loans. Each micro lending entity has its preferred profile. In the United States microloans range from $500 to $25,000, depending on the loan provider.

***When to use a microlender.*** Microloans are an excellent alternative for companies in the early to late start-up phase that have small capital needs but do not qualify for bank financing. Owners may have already tapped into a home's equity or credit cards but need additional capital to grow the business. Entrepreneurs can also use microloan funds to acquire a small business. If an owner is selling a small business for $30,000 and will owner finance $15,000, a microloan of $15,000 would bridge the gap. Microlenders usually do not allow entrepreneurs to use the funds for general working capital, requiring instead that the owner designate a specific usage of the funds.

⸽⟹***Example Four: Microlenders.*** Gloria provided gift baskets to friends, family and co-workers for occasions including hospitalization, birthdays, anniversaries, and celebrations. After receiving continual rave reviews and encouragement, Gloria started a gift basket service. Gloria worked as a teller at a bank and did not make much money. In addition, she only had $300 in savings. To minimize costs, Gloria requested deposits or pre-pays for her gift baskets. This worked for a while. Then one day Gloria received a call from a corporate concierge service inquiring about her gift baskets. The concierge said her baskets had come highly recommended, and he wanted to order ten for a client who wanted to send nice gifts. The concierge faxed over an order request.

Gloria borrowed from friends and family to fulfill the order. When she successfully delivered the baskets, she was paid. Shortly thereafter she began receiving more orders. She realized she could not keep borrowing from friends and family. She found her way by asking around and was directed to a microlender. She completed the application, providing a personal financial statement to serve as notice of her limited collateral. Ultimately, she obtained a microloan for $10,000. Gloria used this loan to fulfill her orders on a timely basis and market her baskets more broadly. Gloria eventually quit her teller job and focused on making and selling baskets full-time.

**Owner financing.** If you are acquiring the stock, shares, membership interests or assets of an existing business, the seller may be willing to finance a portion of the sales price. This is called *owner financing*. With owner financing, the owner takes back a loan on the business. This means the seller holds a note payable to him by the business. You may be able to convince the seller to take back a note for up to 80 to 90% of the purchase price. In this case, you would only have to come up with 10 to 20% of the purchase price to close the transaction.

Sometimes business brokers offer businesses for sale with limited seller financing. Many times businesses are offered for sale with no seller financing expressly stated. However, most small businesses are sold with some seller financing. The percentage of businesses sold with seller financing and the amount of seller financing increases in a market with restricted access to capital as was the case from 2009 to 2012. It is up to you to broach the subject and convince the seller you are a highly credible buyer and that it is in his or her best interest to provide some financing.

The seller understands the business well – better than any bank or other debt source, except perhaps a supplier. Therefore, the seller is the perfect candidate to finance the purchase of the business as long as the business cash flow can support the debt. You must establish a relationship with the seller in order to increase his comfort level. This will lead to an increase in the amount of money he will lend you against the purchase of the business. If you do not possess effective negotiating skills, enlist the services of a broker working on your behalf (brokers are paid by the sellers, usually) or an attorney to negotiate on your behalf. However, you must build the relationship because you will be the one making the payments, not your advisors.

*When to use owner financing.* Pursue some level of owner or seller financing whenever you are pursuing an acquisition.

▶ *Example Five: Seller financing.* John decided to purchase a laundromat. He made everyone aware of his desire and intent, including the members of all the groups he belonged to. A member of his church group, Mary, approached him. Mary had recently retired from her job and wanted to spend more time traveling. However, she spent 20 hours per week at the coin laundry she owned. This prevented her from traveling as freely as she wanted. Mary realized selling the business could also allow her to supplement her retirement income in the same way taking home profits from the business did.

Mary offered to sell her laundromat to John. Since she knew John as an acquaintance for four years, she felt comfortable offering him owner financing when he asked. They agreed on a $200,000 sales price. John had saved $30,000 to put down. Mary agreed to take back two notes, one for $160,000 for seven years at 8.5% per annum and another for $10,000 at 8% per annum for one year. Since Mary only owed $40,000 in outstanding loans on the laundromat, the seller financing presented a viable option for her.

In addition, the monthly payments John made would provide Mary with income to replace the income she received from the laundromat, but without the headache or the 80-hour per month time requirement. Mary intended to use this income to pay her travel expenses and add to her nest egg. John liked the deal because he was able to buy a business at terms similar to a bank, but without the documentation and collateral requirements required by the banks. He also obtained a much higher overall loan-to-value using the seller financing than he would from a bank.

**Purchase order (P/O) financing.** Purchase order financing is significantly harder to obtain than accounts receivable (A/R) financing or factoring. Hundreds, if not thousands, of factoring and A/R firms exist, but only a small number of firms provide P/O financing. With this type of financing, the financing entity uses the purchase order as collateral. Therefore, the P/O must be guaranteed, meaning the customer cannot return the product or demand a refund for the service rendered. Typically, the order must be very large to justify the processing cost and risk involved – at least $50,000 for some, $100,000 for others.

Because of the risks involved, purchase order financing firms will lend only 50% to 60% of the order total. As soon as the order is filled, payment is due to the lender. Some lenders will intercede on the company's behalf instead of funding an order outright, as illustrated in the example below.

***When to use purchase order financing.*** When you must incur a huge cost in advance of creating a receivable and, consequently, cannot utilize accounts receivable financing or factoring because you have no receivables to finance or factor, purchase order financing can provide a good alternative.

⟫ ***Example Six: Purchase order financing.*** Linda, the owner of a four-month old product start-up company, held a $500,000 order from a Fortune 100 firm. She approached Blue Horizon Financial, an asset-based lender and purchase order financing provider, to provide purchase order financing to enable her to fulfill the order. Linda had solicited manufacturers to manufacture her company's product but all demanded upfront payment due to her business' lack of history and financial wherewithal. Of course, Linda did not possess the money to make the upfront payments.

After reviewing Linda's purchase order, production quotes, and the two-page executive summary of the start-up, Blue Horizon Financial agreed to provide the financing to fulfill the order. To directly oversee the product manufacturing and fulfillment process to ensure their monies were not misspent or misdirected, Blue Horizon Financial directly requested the orders from the manufacturers, relegating Linda's small company to the background.

Because Blue Horizon was a reputable company with financial strength, the manufacturers agreed to manufacture the products with payment due in net 30. Since the Fortune 100 customer had agreed to pay upon receipt, this intervention was all that was necessary to obtain the grace period or "financing" necessary to successfully fill the customer's orders. Blue Horizon did not have to actually advance payment to the manufacturer. Therefore, it only charged Linda a small factoring fee to cover the gap between the end of the 30 day period and the actual time that the Fortune 100 firm made payment, a period of less than seven days.

Linda also paid a small fee for Blue Horizon's intervention on her behalf. This and the other financing fee summed to only a small percentage of the amount she would have paid for Blue Horizon to fund the advance payment to the manufacturer. However, Blue Horizon had been fully prepared to make the advance payment.

# CHAPTER 6

# Alternative Lending Sources (Small to Medium Companies)

A true accounts receivable is money due for a product that has been shipped, received, and accepted, or for a service that has been rendered. The receivable is created when the supplier of the product or service invoices the recipient. Accounts receivable financing firms set up a revolving line of credit, using your accounts receivable as collateral, but with little or no involvement with your customers. You continue to own your invoices and you maintain the relationships with your customers.

When a company grows quickly, it occasionally exceeds the limits of its bank lines of credit or other financing and does not yet have the historical financials many banks require to support an increase. In this case, accounts receivable financing can serve as an excellent financing source to bridge the gap. As the company expands, it increases its revenues significantly. These same revenues, via the receivables created, provide the base for the financing, enabling the company to continue its growth trajectory.

***Accounts receivable financing versus factoring?*** The primary difference between accounts receivables financing and factoring is that factoring firms purchase the receivables outright, taking ownership of the receivables. However, A/R financing (aka A/R financing) firms place liens on the receivables but your company retains ownership of those receivables. This means A/Rs still appear as assets on your company's balance sheet. The A/R financing firm then provides a line of credit to your company against those receivables.

In contrast, the factoring firm paid a discount for the receivables. The rates charged typically range from prime +1.5% for lines of credit of $3 million and higher to prime + 3.5% for smaller, less credit-worthy lines of credit. In addition, A/R financing firms charge service fees of 1% to 3% monthly.

***When to use A/R financing.*** A/R financing becomes valuable when you need a line of credit to fund your working capital needs but cannot obtain the financing through a bank. Or, you already have a bank credit line but your business is growing significantly and your bank will not increase your credit line to cover your increased working capital needs.

➡ ***Example Seven: Accounts receivable financing.*** Carver Software was a small company that created software for individuals to manage their personal finances. Carver pursued the military personnel market, both through the government and through the banks that provided banking services to the enlisted military. After months of pursuing contracts, Carver was finally on the verge of winning one with a Georgia Army base. The only catch was that the procurement officer needed proof that Carver had sufficient financially stability to properly service the contract.

Carver's owner contacted Allen of Allen Financial, an accounts receivable financing firm. The owner told Allen that he had a contract if only Carver Software could procure guaranteed funding for the contract.

He asked Allen if Allen Financial could provide a Commitment Letter to extend a line of credit to Carver to service the contract. After analyzing Carver's financials and the owner's credit, reviewing an Executive Summary, reviewing the contract, and knowing the payment history of the army base, Allen issued a Commitment Letter. Allen Financial committed to provide a $200,000 line of credit against the receivables generated by the contract.

Carver presented the Commitment Letter to the procurement officer. Subsequently, the procurement officer awarded the contract to Carver Software, and Allen Financial provided the credit line to service it.

**Equipment financing.** Providers of equipment financing range from small equipment lending entities to large equipment lenders such as Textron Financial, which provides financing and leases on multi-million dollar assets such as airplanes, ships, and helicopters. Equipment lenders include original equipment manufacturers, equipment vendors and distributors, independent leasing companies, and affiliates (usually meaning brokers) that provide financing for the equipment they sell and lease.

Many equipment manufacturers offer built-in financing. They often provide the financing to purchase the equipment outright or provide leasing arrangements. A few providers, primarily distributors, may offer lease-to-own.

Entities that provide equipment loans use the equipment – and rarely much else – as the collateral. Due to the high integrity of the collateral, a non-bank equipment loan typically allows for a lower credit rating and looser operating history than that required by banks. Equipment leasing providers allow even lower credit standards since they retain ownership and your company essentially leases or rents the equipment.

When your company already owns a piece of equipment or maintains a low outstanding balance on the loan against the equipment, it can sell the equipment and lease it back to raise cash for other usages. This is called a sale leaseback. Your company sells the asset to a funding source for cash while simultaneously entering into a contract to lease the asset from that source. One possible drawback is the sales tax usually payable on the sale.

Another option for medium-sized companies with revenues of $10 - $20 million and higher is the *synthetic lease*. A synthetic lease is an operating lease structured so that it is not recorded as a liability on the balance sheet, nor is the corresponding leased asset shown as an asset on the balance sheet. Put another way, a synthetic lease allows a company to **control** assets without showing them on the balance sheet. Instead, the lease is reflected as an expense on the income statement. Both synthetic leases and sale-leasebacks are considered "off-balance sheet" financing. As such, these lease obligations do not increase the debt to equity ratio or reduce the lessee's credit capacity.

***When to use equipment financing.*** Use equipment financing when your company needs to purchase equipment. Use lease financing when your company needs to use an asset for a short-term (e.g., one to four years) or when the lease includes maintenance on the equipment, enabling you to reduce your fixed cost structure. Also when you obtain better terms on a lease than with a purchase, pursue the lease alternative.

➡ ***Example Eight: Equipment financing via leasing.*** Brownmare Bus Lines, with the assistance of Anthony Pace Jr., its CFO, grew to its current size over the last 30 years. Anthony's uncle started the company 30 years earlier to capitalize on the growth of suburbia and the associated increase in movement between the nearby towns. To date, the company owned all of the buses it had purchased to meet the demand.

Anthony reconsidered this policy. With the rise of the immigrant population in the towns they served, the movement patterns changed. The people often rode the bus for shorter trips and complained about the wait. To address the shift, Brownmare decided to purchase smaller, van-sized buses that would make more frequent trips and go shorter distances. However, the CEO and president, Anthony's cousins, were not convinced this strategy would be successful.

To limit their risk, Anthony and his cousins decided to lease ten small buses for one year with the option of renewing for five years or purchasing outright. Thus, Brownmare reduced its typical upfront bus expenditure and lowered its financial risk. The company used the remainder of the cash that had been earmarked for the bus purchase to fund the marketing campaign announcing the availability of the new buses.

**Hard money financing.** Hard money financing entities provide short-term financing, typically 3 to 24 months, for projects, equipment purchases, real estate acquisitions, and purchase of companies. Hard money financing requires collateral in the form of land, real estate, equipment, contractual invoices, or personal assets. Hard money is also sometimes called bridge financing or mezzanine financing. Hard money affords the user time to finalize or deliver upon the conditions that will allow the long-term funding to come in.

Hard money is called such because it *is* short-term and commands higher interest rates, often between nine to 18%. In addition, hard money may charge as many as five points up front. The abbreviated term mandates that the user *must* have a plan B and, hopefully, a plan C to come up with the money to take out the hard money loan in the allotted period of time. Hard money lenders do sometimes grant extensions but these are typically difficult to come by. *Never* assume that the extension request will be granted.

In the case of a real estate project, hard money is usually used when the risk profile of the property is too low for most other lenders to finance. This typically applies to properties that are in very poor physical condition and need extensive renovation, land or physical structures that need environmental remediation, or land that needs to be blasted or backfilled to be suitably usable. In these cases, hard money financing would be used to bring these properties up to a suitable condition where regular bank or other permanent or construction financing could then apply.

Another potential scenario for hard money use related to real estate rehabilitation, conversion, or development projects occurs when there is insufficient investor funding or equity to satisfy the construction loan provider. The hard money lender provides the funds that enable the construction loan to kick in and, hence, construction to commence. Once construction begins, the developer typically has an easier time of garnering investment and finalizing equity infusions from interested parties. The proceeds from the equity infusion or combination equity infusion plus lower interest rate construction loan takes out (pays off) the hard money loan.

***When to use hard money lenders.*** If you have been turned down by traditional banks for any number of reasons and, after further due diligence, you still believe strongly that the project is worth it, then hard many may be your only recourse. Be sure to line up traditional financing to take out the hard money loan even if you intend to sell the entire project upon its completion. Hard money lenders tend to commence foreclosure proceedings faster than traditional banks, so you will want to ensure you are covered (have bought additional time) should your sale fall through. If you are a rapidly expanding company and are pursuing an equity infusion, and if you believe you will successfully close on the transaction within the next 12-18 months (24 months maximum), then pursue hard money financing as a bridge loan. Be sure to structure an equity transaction to take out the hard money loan.

⟶ ***Example Nine: Hard money financing.*** Stephanie, the owner of a small real estate investment company, Smith Family Properties, owners of a few small multi-family properties, decided to pursue the purchase and rehabilitation of single family homes full-time. Stephanie pursued a bank line of credit to fund the purchase and renovation of the properties. However, the company had never obtained loans in the Smith Family Properties' name and so did not possess the credit capacity to obtain a line of credit. Stephanie pursued a construction loan. However, most banks were only interested in extending full construction loans for development purposes with only a small amount allotted for the land purchase. Therefore, the banks were not interested in releasing the larger funds early as required to purchase the houses.

Stephanie then turned to hard money lenders. These lenders were willing to advance the funds to pay off the seller (the purchase funds) and the funds, through a draw down schedule, to pay the renovation and remodeling costs (construction funds). The interest rates and fees were higher, but Stephanie was able to close on each hard money loan within ten days of going into contract on the property.

Since many of the properties' owners or the properties were in dire financial straits, response time was crucial. Using the hard money, Stephanie renovated all of the properties and sold each of them within eight months, well under the 12-month loan term.

**Peer-to-Peer Lending.** One new and growing source of microloans (loan below $50,000) is *peer-to-peer lending* networks. With peer-to-peer lending, also referred to as social lending, providers make direct loans between consumers and investors possible. No third party intermediary exists as it does at a bank where the bank takes deposits then lends those deposits out as loans. Peer-to-peer lending entities connect those who have money to invest with those who need money. These official networks and companies did not exist ten years ago. Social lending is another example of how people and companies continue to engineer creative legitimate solutions to business financing needs.

Peer-to-peer lending provides you with access to a community of peers who serve as lenders to your business without the drawbacks of traditional loans. Peer-to-peer lending entities provide loans by connecting people who want to make a higher return on their money with those who need the money. Individuals can access the money for any purpose including business start-up or expansion funds. These sites provide loans in the name of the individual. The loan is non-recourse meaning that you do not have to put up any collateral for the loan. However, the loan is in your personal name so it will show up on your personal credit report.

Your corporation can also use peer-to-peer lending sites to obtain loans when it does not qualify for bank loans. Before you create your offer, the site will pull your credit score to determine whether you qualify for a loan and, if you do, your interest rate. Just as you would any loan provider, you must specify how much you need, what you need the loan for, what you intend to do with the proceeds, and the term of the loan. You need to make your write-up succinct and compelling. Unlike with a bank or receivables financing firm, you do not have the space to submit an executive summary. The people who are potential funders come from all kinds of backgrounds, most with minimal finance and accounting acumen. Your potential lenders will be drawn by your credit score, the interest rate, the loan's length and your story.

At most peer-to-peer lending sites, investors review the loan listings and invest in those that meet their personal criteria. You can specify if your loan must be 100% funded for you to accept it or if a partial funding, for example, 80%, is acceptable. If you specify full funding and you receive insufficient commitments, then your loan will not fund. Loan requests typically remain listed for 2 to 3 weeks, depending on the size of the loan and your personal preference. The average loan size varies depending on the site.

➤ *Example Ten: Peer to peer lending.* Stephanie White, the founder of TFS Services, Inc. needed $25,000 to retire an IRS bank lien, access marketing services, and cover expenses for three months. She applied for a small business line of credit as a signature loan but was turned down because she had recently quit her job. She remembered reading about peer-to-peer lending. She went to a popular peer-to-peer lending site, read all the information and decided to apply.

Stephanie completed an online application during which time the peer-to-peer lending site pulled her credit and quoted her an interest rate. She then provided a brief written description of why she needed the money and what she intended to do with it. The online signup asked if she wanted "all or nothing" or would be willing to take as little as 60 percent of the requested amount. She indicated she would be willing to take 80 percent but not less if not enough people signed up to fund her. The site noted that her loan request had 21 days to fully fund. Stephanie electronically signed the loan request. She was told that if and when it funded, the funds would directly transfer into her designated checking account within 24 hours of funding.

Once her loan request went live, it took a few days for the first several people to fund. After that, Stephanie's loan fully funded in two more days. All in all, it took less than 6 days. She received a transfer of all the funds within 24 hours, minus the site's fee.

**Supplier or vendor financing**. "Traditional" supplier financing involves stretching out payables from paid upon receipt or net 30 days to 60 to 90 days. Typically, unless agreed upon in advance, suppliers tend to balk on extending terms past 30 days. If your supplier is also a small business, your slow payments could cause it cash flow problems, adversely impacting the supplier, especially if you are a major customer. However, if the supplier is somewhat larger and has good credit, a discussion in advance to extend longer terms due to your inability to obtain a loan or other financing may be just what you need to obtain the longer terms.

If your business has been a good customer or has the likelihood of becoming a larger customer, the supplier may even be willing to provide you with a short- or medium-term loan secured by the inventory or equipment the supplier provides you. The best way to make this happen is to appeal to the supplier's business sense and stress the highly positive impact your business' growth will have on the supplier.

Another means to secure longer terms is to agree to make the supplier the sole or majority supplier of a particular product for a designated period of time, at least the length of the requested loan. You may induce your key supplier to provide you with a term loan of one to three years to finance the purchase of another business or its assets, working capital or expansion capital. The supplier knows the security for the loan – your inventory, his products – well and, therefore, will value the inventory much higher than a bank.

*One caveat.* Large national firms often lack the internal flexibility to negotiate terms with smaller vendors. However, these large companies may contract or sub-contract out to medium-sized firms that do have the internal flexibility. If you think your company could negotiate better terms with a major vendor than with the national firm, you can find that vendor and negotiate directly with it.

*When to use supplier financing.* Use supplier financing when your business relies (or could rely) heavily on one to three suppliers to provide a substantial amount of goods resulting in a significant revenue and profit impact on the suppliers from your business. If your supplier will benefit tremendously from your expansion – for example, their sales or profit will increase in direct proportion to your increase in sales – approach your supplier for a loan. When your supplier is small enough that you can negotiate directly with the owner, president, or general manager of the firm, do so.

*Reputable sources.* Any supplier who stands to reap substantial benefits and possesses the financial wherewithal to provide the loan is a good source of supplier financing. For laundromat owners, most regional equipment distributors provide 50% to 70% of the financing on a new store. They provide similar financing percentages on existing stores when the new owner contracts with them to replace the bulk of the existing washers and dryers. For those owners that successfully utilized the financing before (i.e., those with a track record), the distributors may supply up to 100% financing.

Read the trade journals, industry news, books, and other applicable media to determine what the financing norms are for your industry. Use the norms as a *guide* only. Your supplier's confidence in you, your negotiating skills, your ability to build trust and belief in you, and your account's present and future value are what will ultimately determine your ability to tap into supplier financing.

➠ *Example Eleven: Bank, Seller and Supplier financing.* Ravi owned a thriving package store – a store that sells wines and spirits. He wanted to buy a second store but did not have sufficient funds. He had opened the first store 1.5 years previously and, since the original store was still heavily mortgaged, he could not take on any new loans against his existing store. He had used a bank loan to open the original store. At that time, the bank had placed a second lien on his home and a blanket lien on his current store's equipment and fixtures. His bank agreed to fund $180,000 of the $300,000 purchase price of the second store. However, Ravi could not convince his bank to increase this loan amount to cover the $120,000 shortfall between the agreed-upon purchase price and the bank's term loan. After further negotiation, the seller agreed to hold a note for four years for $50,000, leaving Ravi with a $70,000 shortfall.

Ravi approached his primary liquor wholesaler, Dan. Since Ravi kept good records, he knew how much he spent with this wholesaler. He told Dan that the current owner of the second store bought from Dan's competitor. This competitor made Ravi an offer to help finance the purchase of the second store because he did not want to lose the account. However, Ravi said he wanted to remain with Dan and Dan's company. Yet he did need the loan for $70,000 to provide the financing to cover the shortfall between the sales price and the financing he had already lined up.

Ravi positioned the loan in terms of what Dan stood to gain – a 90 to 100% increase in revenue from Ravi, and intimated what Dan stood to lose – the existing revenue from Ravi and the increase in revenue. After consulting with his business partner, Dan decided to extend Ravi the $70,000 loan at the prime interest rate for three years secured by the wine and spirits inventory Dan's company supplied to Ravi.

▰➡ *Example Twelve: Supplier financing.* A local specialty publishing company began its expansion with annual net income of $175,000. The owner, Heather, decided to acquire complementary service businesses to grow the company and round out its service offering. The company acquired a small graphics firm for $40,000. Heather asked the printer to whom she subcontracted nearly all of her printing work to provide the financing to make the purchase. Given that the work she subcontracted to the printer represented 80% of the printer's revenues, the printer agreed to provide the financing.

Heather's revenues grew with the purchase and she sent even more business to the printer. She then entered into contract to buy a small gift card publishing company that outsourced most of its printing. She again tapped the printer for financing, promising to sub-contract the gift card printing to the printer. The printer provided the $100,000 loan needed to close the transaction. In this way, the company grew into a regional niche publisher with revenues exceeding $3.2 million using only supplier financing.

**Venture merchant banks**. Venture merchant banks fund clients' trade activities such as importing and distribution. They cater to small and midsize businesses with $5 million to $50 million in annual sales. Venture merchant banks offer financing backed by assets, such as purchase orders, accounts receivables and inventory. Relationships with these entities usually last two to three years. At the end of the engagement period, the clients have usually solidified operations and developed enough of a track record to qualify for other forms of financing. Venture merchant banks generally charge 30% of the net income generated during the two to three year period. This fee includes interest charges and fines for late payments.

As with venture capitalists or merchant banks, venture merchant banks take a more interactive role in the management of the company (hence the name "merchant"). They often provide advice and typically manage the client's trade activities during the period of engagement.

This is to ensure the success of the client company which in turn ensures that the venture merchant bank receives an appropriate return on its financing "investment."

**When to use venture merchant banks.** If your company has pursued traditional bank financing, including term loans and lines of credit, SBA-guaranteed loans, factoring firms and accounts receivable financing firms, but has continually been rejected, you should consider venture merchant financing. If your company generates an **absolute** minimum of $1 million (preferably $3 million or more) in annual revenue and has strong purchase orders or contracts in excess of $1 million with reliable customers, then you should pursue venture merchant banks.

Companies that utilize overseas manufacturers or have international customers often encounter resistance from other financing sources. Many U.S. financial institutions lack familiarity or experience with overseas ventures and financing. In this case, assuming your company would fit in the first two scenarios, venture merchant banks may provide the solution to your capital needs.

▶ *Example Thirteen: Venture merchant bank financing.* Amara Apparel, a three-year old specialty apparel company, generated $750,000 in revenue in their third year of operation and was on track to double that revenue the following year. The company participated in a number of tradeshows and expositions that generated large orders. Tracee Amara, the company's founder, found herself in a quandary with the increasing order size. She encountered cash flow challenges in trying to ramp up personnel and internal operational support systems to meet the demand. She also had to pay her suppliers in net 30 days, but typically did not receive payment for her company's wares until 70 days after she placed the order, resulting in a cash flow gap.

Tracee pursued factoring and accounts receivable financing to no avail. Because her manufacturers were based in China and India and nearly half of her customers were based in the Middle East, France, and England, few felt comfortable taking on the "international" risk.

That, coupled with the fact that her company was still in an early stage, resulted in repeated denials of financing. Tracee grew very concerned that her company would grow itself out of existence due to its inability to obtain financing.

With no more options, Tracee began to tell others about Amara Apparel's situation and ask for assistance. A friend of a friend recommended venture merchant financing. Tracee had never heard of it and did not know where to turn, so she headed to the library and Internet to do some research on the subject. Tracee then called larger financial advisors and a couple of respected local merchant bankers to ask them to recommend a venture merchant bank. Once connected, it took six weeks to arrange a meeting and finalize the negotiations. Through the venture merchant bank she secured financing totaling $4 million over three years.

# PART II

# EQUITY FINANCING SOURCES

# CHAPTER 7

# Equity Financing Sources – Overview

For many start-ups and growing companies, equity is often the optimal funding choice. Why? Because the companies find it very difficult to obtain debt financing OR the company cannot generate the cash flow to service the debt. In the latter case, a good company could quickly experience financial distress due to an improper or inadequate capital structure. A rapidly growing company carrying too much debt needs to retire debt and infuse equity.

Using equity financing does have some drawbacks. Equity is generally considered an expensive source of capital because equity investors typically require rates of return of 20 to 40% annually. Compare this to banks which typically charge only 7% to 12% typically. Equity investors often require a board seat. In addition, equity investors' proportionate stake in the company reduces the founders' stake (also known as share dilution).

However, equity possesses a number of significant advantages. Equity can be extremely flexible. For example, a company may delay payouts for several years, allowing time for the company to grow into a stronger cash position. Equity can be used to enhance borrowing capacity since it strengthens the balance sheet. It provides capital for growth without fixed payments. Finally, the equity investor(s) may provide a wealth of ideas, contacts, business acumen and other opportunities that a company would have to pay for or access through other means, if at all.

For all private sources of equity, it is crucial to find investors who share the vision for the growth and direction of the company. Since these entities will have significant ownership stakes, they typically will have one or more board seats and pronounced voting impact. Essentially, these entities or their representatives will be a *de facto* member of the management team. If the goals of the investors do not align with those of the founders and company management, the company's growth will likely falter. If the relationship derails beyond the point of no return, depending on the terms of the investment agreement and the ownership stake of the firm, the investors could force out the company's current management.

You must properly structure your company for equity investment. If you intend to sell shares to multiple investors, you should choose a corporate legal structure for your company over a limited liability company (LLC). LLCs do not allow the flexibility of share structure (i.e., preferred class A, preferred class B, common) that corporations allow. Angels, venture capitalists, and private equity investors typically need to ensure that they are re-paid before any of the owners or founders of the business or before the company uses money for other non-essential expenses. Therefore, they typically demand preferred treatment for their investment funds, represented by preferred shares.

In addition, you must structure (or re-structure) the company to allow the issuance of ten million or more shares. The shares will not be issued at once but will be issued as new equity financing is obtained. If you only have 1,000 shares and you issue 800 to you and your relatives, you only have 200 to issue to outside investors. That would be totally unacceptable to any interested sophisticated investor.

(However, this may be fine for your friends and family whose focus is on supporting you.)

You can see clearly how this transforms into a very unwieldy situation in no time. How would the follow-on investors obtain shares in the company? Consult with a corporate or small business attorney to set up your corporate structure and designate the appropriate number of shares. If you have already formed a corporation with 10,000 shares, consult the attorney to make the requisite changes and amend your corporate documents.

Equity investors are there to make money on their investment. Some investors are very hands off and serve as advisors or relationship connectors when needed. Others are very involved and actively participate in driving company growth. Companies need to be aware of the type of investor the equity provider is – for example, detached, actively involved, or somewhere in the middle. For those companies that have been sorely lacking a strong advisory board, a highly active investor may be just what the business needs to catapult the company into high-level growth. In the end, the decision rests with the owners. Therefore, owners seeking equity must clearly understand the mission of the company, the goals of the company in terms of growth, market focus, market penetration, the uses of the capital and the exit strategy.

Because of this, I highly recommend documentation such as Private Placement Memorandums (PPMs). The process of compiling this and similar documents requires company owners and management to identify their needs, wants, and desires in order to clearly delineate the information in the documentation. Since the owner has already thought a lot of things through, when interested investors are found, the negotiation process goes much faster and smoother.

All equity investors envision an exit – most within seven years. Therefore, you must think clearly about what the best exit strategy is for the investors you will target for your company. You should also have your own personal exit strategy. Should you own a viable business that you intend to grow into a larger and even more sustainable corporation, you need to think of your company as a long-term investment that creates wealth for you and your family, any partners or co-founders, and any current and future investors.

Exit strategies vary. If you intend to pass your business down to your children or other relatives, you will completely avoid some exit strategies and strongly prefer others. If you intend to grow the business and eventually hand over the business to professional management, the board of directors, and shareholders/investors, but intend to remain at the helm until you approach early or regular retirement age, you will have a vastly different exit strategy focused on decreasing your ownership stake over time and obtaining the large amounts of capital needed to expand a business to several hundred million or more in revenue. If you would simply like to hold the business as a good investment, great income source, and grow it to a comfortable size before selling out, your exit strategy will differ still.

Exit strategies for owners and investors include IPOs, private placements or private stockholder purchases (where shares in a closely held corporation are sold to up to 35 accredited investors), and merger with or acquisition by another (usually larger) firm. Exit strategies for investors only include corporate buybacks (where the company recapitalizes the business, usually with debt, and buys back the investors' shares with cash), venture capital (where an angel's shares are purchased in a follow-on round by venture capitalists) or the sale of the appreciated shares to another investor. Owners can either sell the firm outright to another individual or entity or sell his or her proportionate stake in the firm. Following an IPO, an owner can sell down their stake in the firm in the public markets.

**Pursuing equity**. When pursuing equity, prepare a brief PowerPoint presentation of 12-15 slides that takes approximately six to eight minutes to present. Investors want to hear you speak about your business. Investors look for deep knowledge of the industry and the market, understanding of how your product or service addresses the need or "pain points" in a market and a strong, recognizable competitive advantage. They also look for passion. Passion means different things for different personality types, but no matter if you are the classic nerd or the gregarious salesman, passion comes through.

You should also prepare a one-page profile on your company which condenses the information contained in the Executive Summary. You can use this document to pique someone's interest enough for her to request the Executive Summary or other, more detailed documentation. If you do not have these documents, there are many consultants, coaches and advisors who can assist you in the preparation of these documents or point you to online resources and books to try to create it yourself.

Remember, when pursuing financing, you are selling your company, not your product. Focus on the components of the business that make your company stand out. Examples include the following: $x$ number of customers signed up in $y$ short period of time; highly experienced management team; involvement of serial entrepreneur; market size; current market share (if significant); acquisition candidates; realistic profit projections; and/or employee contributions.

Do not exclusively focus, as so many entrepreneurs do, on the great idea, product, or service you have. Instead, focus primarily on the pain points in your targeted market that your product or service mitigates or eradicates. Sometimes companies must drastically modify their product and service offerings to meet the needs of a changing market. You want to communicate that you stay abreast of the market and have the management know-how to take the necessary actions to grow the business and weather the challenges that will come your way.

CHAPTER 8

# Equity Financing
# Sources (Small Businesses)

A ngel investors are individuals or groups of individuals who invest, passively or actively, in small, privately held businesses. They are called "angels" because they provide the funding to move the company to the next level when many other entities such as banks or other equity providers such as VCs and private equity firms still consider the firm too risky. In other words, they are often the answer to many small companies' prayers! According to the Center for Venture Research, in 2012 angels invested $22.9 Billion in 67,030 ventures; in 2005 angels invested $23.1 Billion in 49,500 companies.

**Angel investors.** Angel investors should be accredited investors. To qualify as an accredited investor, a person exhibits one of the following:

1. Have an individual annual income in excess of $200,000 for the last two years, or have a joint income with their spouse of $300,000 over the same time frame;

2. Have a net worth of $1 million; or

3.  Be a director, officer, or general partner of the entity issuing the securities.

If you pursue someone as an angel investor who does not meet the monetary criteria in items 1 or 2, then you must structure the investment to include the investor as a director or officer of the company. Otherwise, utilize a Private Placement Memorandum (described in detail in the next chapter) to solicit investment from non-accredited investors.

There are many people who don't call themselves angels. Often these individuals say they want to acquire little pieces of smaller companies, or they want to invest in one company and run it or actively participate on the board. Because they just don't know, or because they associate angels only with the dot-com era and high tech companies, these individuals just don't refer to themselves as angels. Angels are often lawyers, doctors, financial managers, senior management-level executives, business owners and former entrepreneurs. All angels are much more likely to invest in the companies of those they know personally or that were referred to them through a trusted source such as their lawyer, accountant or financial planner.

Many angels are hidden in plain sight – you just do not know who has the money to invest. So, make no assumptions. Keeping in mind that prospective angels may not be readily apparent, you can find angels via the following: angel networks (e.g., Atlanta Technology Angels or ATA), acquaintances and relatives of friends and family, associations and clubs (especially professional associations or higher-cost activity clubs such as ski clubs or country clubs), school alumni or alumni associations, church members, and occasionally websites.

Websites are the least likely because money is usually provided only after the cultivation of a relationship. If someone referred you to an angel, the relationship was already established through the referring entity. If you met the person directly and interested this person in your business, you have a relationship. Sending an executive summary blindly through a website solicitation process is similar to applying for a job through the Internet. It can work, but it is much more of a numbers game and will likely take some time unless your Executive Summary and business truly stand out from the crowd.

A number of the highly active investors have built and sold at least one company. Often they have built two or more companies before they actually became active investors. An active investor wants to give back by helping another entrepreneur build a company and create jobs.

Be wary of the unsophisticated "newbie" angel. Inexperienced angels can create management headaches and interfere with later funding rounds. Be sure to think mid-term and long-term, not just short-term, regarding your capital needs.

Usually a company growing at a rapid rate will grow beyond the ability of the angels to fund the company's growth. The later rounds will dilute the ownership percentage of the angels. Therefore, you must structure the deal for the angels to enable them to cash out with the infusion of additional cash or limit their ability to hinder later funding rounds. If the earlier stage financing was structured correctly, despite the angel's dilution, the company should achieve a higher valuation with the new cash infusion. This will maintain, if not increase, the angel's monetary stake in the business. Again, comprehensive deal structuring points to the need for a PPM, as mentioned earlier.

All investors expect to get a return on their investment. Therefore, some will incorporate terms into the agreement to ensure that if your growth does not meet the targets, they gain more and more control.

**When to use angel investors:** You need $25,000 to $1.5 million in financing. If you are in the "seed" pre-revenue stage but you have a working demo or a strong management team track record, and you have several interested prospective customers, then you will appeal to angel investors who want to play an active role in the building of your company. Otherwise, use angels after you gain customers and revenue. One wealthy angel can typically provide smaller amounts of money, i.e.,

$200,000 and less. For more than that, you usually must tap several angels or one or two angel groups.

**Resources.** For more information on locating angel investors and angel investor networks, refer to the Angel Capital Association (ACA) at www.angelcapitalassociation.org. This replaces Active Capital (formerly known as Capital Electronic Network (ACE-Net)), which was previously administered by the SBA in connection with the SEC.

For most of the angel investor groups listed on ACA businesses must meet criteria and pay fees (~$100 to $300 on average) to apply to for investment consideration. Some groups charge additional fees, up to ~$500, to present. Business must submit their Executive Summary and request for funds to the appropriate angel group. The group's staff and a pool of accredited investors (called Angels) review business plans, proposals, and need. Businesses can raise up to $5 million. However, $1 million is the best target for funding for most groups, unless the group is large or very wealthy. The average financing procured under the predecessor, Active Capital, per company was $1.2 million but now the average depends on the group.

➠**Example Fourteen: Strategic investor and Angel financing.** FranchiseWise, a three-year-old company that provides operational and cash management software to franchisees, needed capital to fund working capital needs and to expand its marketing and sales functions. Two years earlier, using contacts in the Filipino business community, the company successfully obtained a strategic $400,000 investment by a Filipino-owned IT staffing company. In exchange for the investment, FranchiseWise agreed to hire (or recommend hiring of) the IT staffing company for all of its software installations.

Working through the franchisors, FranchiseWise successfully closed contracts with a number of franchisees. Dan, the company's president, did not want to use factoring, except where necessary, because the company still had R&D needs. Debt or debt-like alternatives would place too high a burden on the company's cash flows. So Dan and the rest of the management team and advisory board opted to pursue angel investors.

The founders originally organized FranchiseWise as an LLC due to the similarity of treatment of an LLC to a corporation, the low number of investors, and the ease of formation. The company enlisted a service provider to help prepare them for presentations and to shop their deal to various angel investors. However, the company's legal structure presented a huge barrier to angels once the company started its campaign. Angels would initially express interest. Then, immediately after investors were told FranchiseWise was an LLC, investors' interest would plummet. Upon investigation, the founders discovered that angels possessed a significantly higher comfort and familiarity level with C-corporation structures which readily allow for issuance of more than one type of stock such as preferred stock and common stock.

Although the service provider prepared Dan and his team for presentations, the provider did not raise any funds. So Dan and team decided to go it alone. They sent their one-page summary sheets and executive summaries to Atlanta-based and Virginia-based technology-focused angel groups. At first, the groups were not interested but, with persistence and a good word put in by another entity, a Virginia-based angel group brought FranchiseWise in to make a presentation. The Virginia firm made a tentative decision to invest, contingent upon FranchiseWise interesting another angel group in investing.

Dan leveraged this commitment into a meeting with a high-tech incubator with strong ties to the Atlanta-based angel group. The incubator mandated that FranchiseWise convert to a corporation with a sufficient common and preferred stock subscription amount before it would seriously consider accepting the company into its incubation program and helping it obtain additional investment. FranchiseWise complied, converting to a C-corporation with 10 million shares of common stock and 1 million shares of preferred stock.

FranchiseWise subsequently presented to the Atlanta-based angel group and procured equity investments of $850,000 total from the Atlanta and Virginia groups. Subsequently the incubator accepted FranchiseWise into its program. The following year the company nearly tripled its revenue.

**Equity crowdfunding.** Equity crowdfunding is the pooling of monies together from a number of individuals to support a business in exchange for an eventual financial return. Under the federal JOBS Act, the federal government enacted new laws or rules that became effective in September 2013 that allow companies to equity crowdfund to accredited investors on a Securities and Exchange Commission-approved website /platform. Companies can sell up to $1 million in securities or raise up to $1 million in capital from an unlimited number of accredited investors via this method. Instead of obtaining $50,000 from one or two investors, you would get $50,000 from 100 or more investors.

In 2014, the SEC will implement new rules, which are still being defined, that allow non-accredited investors to invest in companies via equity crowdfunding portals. This would enable non-accredited investors to invest small amounts in your company. You could foreseeably have 1,000 investors who all invest $1,000 each. The SEC is allowing this because of the smaller size. Typically, angel groups require a minimum $25,000 investment. Usually as a company seeking financing, it is much easier to obtain large amounts of money from fewer investors, especially if you live in an area where an active angel investment community does not exist. Due to the size of the investments, unsophisticated investors could lose significantly more than they could afford to lose.

Now, with the advent of equity crowdfunding platforms, you can expose your business to thousands or hundreds of thousands of individuals at once, decreasing the time it takes you to find interested investors. In addition, the platform enables you to explain your offering all at once, not piecemeal to 50 different people over the course of six months! All of these individuals can invest as little as the platform allows, which translates into amounts that most middle class individuals feel comfortable with.

To use equity crowdfunding, you will need to prepare the same type of information you would prepare for both presenting to angel investor groups and following up on any inquiries from interested parties. You will need a one-page summary sheet on your company, an investor presentation, and an executive summary.

Once you get to the stage where one or more seriously consider investing, a strategic and operational business plan will add significant credibility to your venture. You should also compile information that verifies some or all of the data you submit. For example, if you say your company generated $2 million in revenue, you should submit tax returns or reviewed or audited financials to substantiate that your company actually generated that amount.

If your company recently jumped to those levels and, therefore, you don't have the financial statements or tax return proof beyond your Quickbooks printout, you can provide bank statements, customer payment receipts or contracts as evidence. Potential investors will need to know that you are legitimate. To comply with SEC regulations, most platforms will request information like this in advance of your posting. Most will also provide you with free assistance in the form of videos and articles to help you prepare the information you need to pursue funding on their site. The more supporting information you compile from a potential investor's perspective, and the more compelling and succinct that information is, the more quickly you will attract funding. The recommendations I give here are not absolute requirements, but they greatly enhance your chances of getting the money you need in a faster time frame.

To use equity crowdfunding, research and seek out those platforms which provide a good fit for your business. Some platforms serve all businesses seeking to raise money, but many others focus on specific industry or sub-industry niches, for example, technology, biotechnology, business services or consumer products. Examine the information to determine how helpful that platform or website will be in helping you package your solicitation. If you need a great deal of help, choose a site that walks you through everything. If you do not, choose a site that appears to be aimed at larger, or more sophisticated, small companies.

Look at the data available on the site or in articles or press releases about the site. Ask yourself, "How successful are they at helping companies raise money?" "What percentage of companies successfully raise money on this site?" "What is the average investor return for investors on this site?" Because of the nascent nature of equity crowdfunding, little data on some of the questions may be available. However, as time progresses and this new sub-industry matures, the data will become increasingly available.

‣ *Example Fifteen: Equity crowdfunding.* Co-founders Joshua Small and Mark Johns created a sunglasses company, Sun Optical, with an eclectic flavor. In keeping with that "flavor," they used guerilla marketing tactics to get the word out about their products and get the company's name in the media. They had achieved, consistent year over year growth in revenue and now needed money to expand their marketing, sales and production efforts.

Joshua and Mark had already tapped their savings, family and friends, and a bank loan to get Sun Optical to this point. They decided they needed equity to get them to the next level. Equity would not strain their cash flow because they would not need to pay it back. However, Joshua and Mark did not have strong relationships with the angel investment community and did not want to spend the next year looking for funding as that would move their attention away from growing the business.

They did some research and approached a well-recognized consumer products-focused equity crowdfunding company. Once Sun Optical successfully passed the screening for that platform, which only accepts ~2% of the companies that apply, the equity crowdfunder helped them raise money in several ways. It obtained press coverage for them in a leading industry publication, connected them with a member of the executive management team at a large consumer products company, and connected them with a strategic investor with experience in the industry.

Sun Optical raised over $800,000 through the equity crowdfunding platform. Through this platform it also attracted individuals who could provide much needed business acumen and insights to serve on the Sun Optical's Advisory Board.

**Joint Ventures.** A joint venture or strategic alliance is a form of partnership where businesses come together to share knowledge, markets and profits. Joint ventures can take on various forms. Small companies can band together to take on the goliaths of their industry. Big companies can form alliances with quicker and nimbler small businesses, and small companies have the opportunity to forge strategic alliances with big name companies for expanded geographic reach.

The golden impact of joint ventures on a firm's bottom line is significant. With joint ventures, you achieve the following:

- *Shorten the Learning Curve:* Building knowledge can be time-consuming and costly.
- *Enhance Company Credibility:* All businesses struggle with building acceptance. A key alliance with a larger company that has a known brand can dramatically improve your credibility.
- *Create New Profit Channels:* Businesses have limited resources and capital. By joint venturing, your small company can expand its sales force and distribution channel without utilizing its own capital.
- *Build Competitor Barriers:* A strategic alliance with several key players can erect impenetrable walls, keeping out competitors and maintaining high profit margins.

Additional financial benefits of joint ventures include financial support or sharing of economic risk, acceleration of revenue growth, and the ability to increase profit margins by tapping into additional resources with minimal expenditures. Other business benefits include the development or acquisition of marketing or distribution expertise and the combination of complementary R&D or technologies.

The latter is often observed among technology companies where customers perceive two separate software products much more highly if the products have the ability to easily integrate with one another. An effective integration plug-in or template is often developed through a partnership between the two firms.

A smaller firm can garner financing via joint ventures by utilizing the credit, banking, and other financial relationships of a larger, stronger joint venture partner to qualify for financing. For example, a smaller or younger company in a construction-related industry can utilize the bonding capacity of a construction partner to build its own bonding capacity and relationships. A firm with minimal internal operational support that anticipates difficulty in getting timely payments from large customers can funnel contractual payments through a partner.

Finally, a small company can obtain an equity investment from its larger or more profitable strategic partner through a direct investment or through a proportionately larger investment in the formal joint venture.

The secrets of successful joint ventures are as follows:

1. **Set Clear Goals.** Know from the beginning what you want to accomplish. Is it reduced product costs, expanded sales, or market credibility? Your partners' goals may be different but complementary to yours.

2. **Find a Partner.** The best partnership is based on a mutual win-win relationship. Take the time to locate a company with an honest interest in joint ventures and a similar corporate

culture. If your small business is focused on long-term customer relations and your strategic partner cares about gaining market share quickly, then your two cultures may clash.

3. **Plan the Venture.** Map out your negotiation tactics and understand the legal aspects of the deal. Keep a win-win agreement in mind.

4. **Manage the Relationship.** Once you form a winning joint venture the real work takes place. A good alliance is like a marriage; it is built on communication, trust and understanding.

### *An example: Real estate.*

Real estate financing entities (banks, insurance companies, private individuals) often enter into joint ventures with experienced developers to undertake residential or commercial development projects. In these situations, the financing entities typically provide a disproportionate amount of the capital required and arrange the financing for the project; the joint venture partner manages the development process and day-to-day operations. The capital commitment can range from $1 to $5 million, higher or lower, depending on the financing entity and the project. The project's success determines the ultimate returns to the developer and to the financing entity.

A joint venture is a financing arrangement whereby the lender receives a portion of the income from operations and from the sale of the building or project. The joint venturer advances the loan funds and puts up a portion of the required equity in return for income and equity participation. This typically occurs at a higher percentage than would be the case under a simple income-equity participation loan due to the added riskiness to the lender of the equity investment portion.

***When to use joint ventures.*** If you need a mentor, additional resources, or capacity, and if you can identify a firm in your industry, you should consider a joint venture partner. Alternatively, if you can find a firm in a complementary industry that you could benefit from and assist, then a joint venture is an excellent way to procure financing or access to otherwise expensive financing.

*Reputable sources.* This depends on the company and the industry. If you are an SBA 8a company, which means that you are certified by the Small Business Administration as a disadvantaged business under a business development program that renews every three years up to nine years, check with your assigned SBA business development officer for suggestions. As an 8a company, the SBA will work with you to craft the joint venture agreement, and will then monitor the relationship. If you are an active participant in a Fortune 500 company's supplier development program or Mentor Protégé program, ask the program head for suggestions. If you belong to industry trade associations, make it known that you seek a partner.

▸ *Example Sixteen: Joint venture financing.* Moove Staffing, a small 8a-certified staffing firm with $3 million in annual sales, wanted to pursue a large federal staffing contract. Sandy, Moove's CEO, estimated the contract would pay $15 million per year for the next three years. Moove did not have the structural or financial capacity to handle this contract amount if it won. Sandy also felt Moove had a number of operational issues she needed to address.

Sandy discussed her options with her strategic advisor, Dawn, a representative of a Minority Business Enterprise Center (MBEC). Dawn's recommendation to Sandy was a joint venture with another of the MBEC's clients, also a staffing firm, but one with $72 million in sales. The other client primarily focused on Fortune 1000 companies as customers and would, therefore, have interest in a segue into the government market.

Dawn contacted the other client, NBV Inc., and arranged a meeting to discuss a joint venture. In the meeting, NBV's CEO, Ken, agreed to the joint venture. In doing so, Ken offered to serve as Sandy's business mentor, provide financing to service the contract, and lend resources to help Sandy strengthen Moove's operational infrastructure. In exchange, NBV would service $12 million of the contract the first year, $8 million the second year, and $2 million the third year. NBV would leverage the relationships built through the contract opportunity to build stronger relationships with sister agencies and obtain more federal government business.

Dawn drew up the formal SBA joint venture documents, obtained signatures from both parties, and submitted the documents to Moove's SBA Business Development Officer for approval. When the SBA approved the joint venture, Dawn helped Sandy prepare the proposal to pursue the $45 million contract opportunity. Although the joint venture lost that bid, it won a subsequent two-year, $32 million contract opportunity with another agency.

**Personal investment.** I assume that you have already tapped your personal resources to fund the business or decided that this is not a viable option (i.e., too much risk or nothing available). However, it does deserve mention. If your company is in an early stage or in a rapid expansion stage, you do not need to load your company with debt provided by you via a shareholder loan to the company. This weakens your balance sheet and that will work against you when pursuing bank loans and other forms of external debt. Hence, I address personal investment in the equity section. If you do not wish to contribute all of your savings or you do not have it to invest in your company, consider taking out a line of credit on your home, obtaining a loan on your fully paid vehicle, or tapping your 401K through a loan and investing the proceeds into your business.

Refer below to other options related to the use of brokerage security accounts, pension funds, and IRAs.

***When to use personal investments***. Invest your personal funds, as much as you can reasonably afford, if you do not have much savings, investments, or home equity. Bootstrapping requires you to focus intently on your business and use as many non-monetary resources as possible to get you to the revenue generation stage and then to profitability as soon as possible.

If you do have significant savings, invest as much as needed to obtain a loan or attract outside capital. Using outside capital often mandates the maintenance of books and the creation of a business plan, all of which makes you hold yourself and your business to a higher operating standard. If you have too much money and too little business operating acumen, you could mismanage the company and lose all you have.

▨▶*Example Seventeen: Personal investment.* Steve Jobs and Steve Wozniak founded Apple Computer in Jobs' garage while Jobs worked as an employee of Atari. Jobs funneled much of the money from his paychecks into buying parts and hiring engineers to construct their prototype computer. They built the first Apple computer in 1976.

Phillip Knight and William Bowerman, Knight's college track coach, started Nike in the early 1960s with $1,000. They sold imported Japanese sneakers from the back of their cars until they generated sufficient interest to obtain contracts and space in retail locations.

**Strategic investors.** Strategic investors are entities that directly derive pronounced benefits from the product or service your company offers. These entities could be existing or targeted partners, customers, suppliers, or complementary service or product providers. The common link is that your company's business will in some way strongly impact the entity's business, hence the 'strategic' designation. These entities stand to profit greatly from the development of your company, *not* just from the increase in your company's revenue or profitability. Typically, a strategic investor would take an equity stake in your business or provide blended equity and debt capitalization.

**When to use strategic investors.** Companies seeking equity investment for a service or product that has a direct impact on a niche market frequently have an interest in finding a strategic investor. So too do companies that have a rapid growth trajectory that may fall short of that sought by angel investment groups, angel networks or venture capitalists.

> **For more articles on strategic investment and strategic investors, visit www.Cash4Impact.com.**

➥ *Example Eighteen: Strategic investor financing.* A medical imaging company, Medical Imaging, Inc., that provides imaging technology over the Internet via a secure network needed financing so that it could grow. A medical imaging technician would upload the photos to the website, then a certified technician would log on from the company's headquarters or from a remote site, assess the images and document his or her comments regarding what he or she observed in the images. The technician would then e-mail a link to these assessed images to the patient's physician to review and discuss with the patient.

Medical Imaging, Inc. needed funds primarily for marketing and business development but also for continued product development. The founder and majority owner, Derek, had procured seed financing when he started the company and had later obtained a round of angel financing. However, to grow the company Derek sought $3 million in capital, larger than the amount that typical angel investors and angel investment groups provide. Derek initiated contacted with venture capital firms but was soon disgusted with the reception he received and the perceived run around to which he was subjected.

Derek was told his company had a good concept and decent revenues (~$2.5 million) but as of yet did not have the stellar growth potential venture capitalists seek for their investments. He received this message repeatedly, in various forms. Admittedly, his arrogant demeanor may have also turned off some of the venture capitalists. Venture capitalists like companies with management that it perceives as coachable. Arrogance and coachability reside on opposite sides of the receptivity spectrum.

During his pursuit, Derek let his large customers and technician providers know of his dilemma – insufficient financing to properly grow the company. One of the customers, a medical group of over 50 heart surgeons, expressed interest in investing in the company. This customer had a highly strategic relationship to the business, more of a strategic partner than a pure customer. Because there was a shortage of imaging specialists, the surgeons' group used the services of the company to drastically reduce the time needed to obtain reviewed images.

The surgeons' group saw this as an excellent way to make the existing technicians more accessible and more efficient. The group therefore entered into discussions to invest in Medical Imaging, Inc. and ultimately invested over $500,000 in the company. Another customer group with strategic ties invested a similar amount in the company. As a result, Derek turned his efforts completely away from venture capitalists to focusing on procuring another large investment from an entity that stood to benefit significantly from the company's services and anticipated growth.

CHAPTER 9

# Equity Financing Sources (Medium-Sized Businesses)

These barely regulated pools of leveraged equity now boast more than $1 trillion in assets. Once reserved for very high net worth individuals due to their minimum investments of $10 million, the number of funds and the amounts invested in hedge funds have grown tremendously. This growth is due to the increase in the ranks of the very wealthy, the disenchantment with the stock market after the tech bubble burst, and the reduction in the minimum investment threshold to as low as $250,000 for some funds. With so much money (and relatedly, so much competition for deals), hedge funds must continually search out new investment vehicles. As a result, more and more hedge funds are investing in or interested in investing in early-stage, (small, high growth potential companies).

**Hedge funds (via IPOs).** According to a January 2006 *Inc.* magazine article, approximately $3 billion in private investments in public equities (PIPEs) was put into more than 300 companies with annual revenues under $5 million. PIPEs, a little known, complex financial vehicle, enable publicly traded companies to sell stock to accredited investors at discounted prices. These publicly traded companies are typically small (revenues of $2 - $10 million) and medium-sized (in terms of capitalization) firms that trade over the counter (OTC). Most of the companies that obtain funding through PIPEs go public by listing on the OTC Bulletin Board in the U.S. via a reverse merger, or by listing on the AIM, the London Stock Exchange's international market for smaller growing companies in the United Kingdom.

Obtaining PIPE financing is significantly more complex and expensive than pursuing equity growth capital through venture capital funds or angels. It requires a "road show." A roadshow is a series of meetings with and presentations to potential investors and brokers conducted by a company and its underwriter prior to a security offering such as an IPO. In the case of a PIPE roadshow, the company travels around the country with an investment banker or other knowledgeable securities advisor presenting directly to numerous hedge fund managers or their representatives.

The banker or advisor is responsible for establishing the relationships and handling of the logistics of the road show. However, it is still a time consuming process for the company owner. Anyone considering the PIPE route **must** enlist the services of a skilled advisor who is highly experienced in this area. The process will cost $200,000 to $700,000 in accounting and legal fees plus an additional 3-5 times this amount for investment banking fees. Despite the cost, for some high-growth potential companies who intend to go public at some stage, this is a highly viable source of funds.

*When to use hedge funds and PIPEs.* Your company has a rapid growth initiative, generates minimum revenues of $2 to $5 million, needs millions to grow as planned, and has intentions of going public.

▰▶ *Example Nineteen: PIPE/Hedge fund financing.* Joe Abrams, the co-founder and CEO of Allied Mortgage Services, a mortgage brokerage specializing in serving buyers of homes priced at $300,000 and above, needed expansion capital. Allied Mortgage had grown from $0 in revenue to $3.5 million in annual sales in 18 months. Joe co-owned the company with his brother and father. Although mortgage brokering is perceived as a high cash business, brokers must pay fixed overhead such as rent and utilities.

Brokers must also pay variable expenses, such as marketing and advertising expenses, fees to loan processors, and fees to other service providers including attorney and appraisers. When a loan closes on a home, the broker receives reimbursement for many of the variable costs at closing plus revenue from both the homebuyer and the lender.

Since re-financings often took two weeks to close, Allied preferred these deals over home purchases. Home purchase loans occasionally took 60-90 days to close. Allied envisioned expansion from a small regional presence in Michigan, Wisconsin, and parts of Canada to a large regional presence in the Midwest and Central Canada. Joe and his family pictured growing Allied to $50 Million in revenue in five years. However, they could not procure more than a $350,000 line of credit for Allied due to the company's age and sales history. Nor did Allied have receivables or other assets it could finance.

Joe and his family determined that an equity infusion was the best way to grow the company. They considered private equity but did not think Allied, as a brokerage, was a good fit. Joe had an MBA from the University of Chicago, and consequently had a lot of former classmates at a number of financial institutions. Joe contacted a few of these classmates for their input. He considered a private placement but decided he needed more money than he could likely raise as the firm was too small and too young to garner the attention of the institutional investors. He had read about the rise in hedge funds over the last several years and asked a classmate about them.

After some discussion, Joe decided to tap into the hedge fund investment community to grow his family's company. He hired a boutique investment banking firm his classmate recommended. After nine months, Allied went public by listing on the OTC BB (Bulletin Board), raising $8 Million for expansion. In the two years following the IPO, Allied grew to $40 Million in revenue and was bought out by a large financial services firm that provided other services to Allied's niche market.

⥤*Example Twenty: Venture capital and PIPE/Hedge fund financing.* Gill Hurt founded Pharmed, a pharmaceutical-coated device manufacturer, ten years before in Radnor, Pennsylvania. Recently, Gill had won a few large contracts with distributors and medical device manufacturers in the United States and Europe. He needed cash to expand Pharmed's facilities in Radnor, hire sales staff, and add operational support to fill the orders. Gill had previously raised $3.5 million from venture capitalists who, when approached for more money, were now reluctant to provide follow-on funding.

One of the venture capitalists who sat on the board recommended that Gill pursue a PIPE. The investor connected him with an investment banking advisor that specialized in PIPEs. Gill liked the prospect of an IPO at an earlier stage because it would result in less dilution and provide direct access to the capital markets. Gill decided to pursue a PIPE. The advisor located a public shell company that had been defunct for the last five years. Pharmed merged into this shell, then listed on the OTC BB under a new ticker, PHMD.OB. Subsequently, Gill's advisor pursued hedge funds.

The investment bank matched Pharmed with over 30 hedge funds. With his investment banker guiding and advising him, Gill made most of the presentations to the hedge fund managers. Two separate fund managers, one in the United Kingdom and one in the United States, joined forces and led the negotiation of terms. Six other hedge funds and seven other accredited investors rounded out the group that provided the $10.5 million in financing to Pharmed seven months after its OTC listing.

The accounting, legal, and other fees for the reverse merger and PIPE transaction plus the investment banking fees totaled $1.4 million. The $1.4 million in fees came out of the $10.5 million financing raised. Pharmed also spends over $30,000 annually to comply with Sarbanes-Oxley and SEC reporting requirements. However, Gill believes it was well worth it. Pharmed's performance exceeded expectations and now lists on Nasdaq. Gill anticipates Pharmed will need additional expansion capital in a year. He will use the same investment bank to make a secondary offering using traditional methods.

**Initial Public Offerings (IPOs).** Initial public offerings are the initial or first sale of stock to the public. IPOs are a way to "go public" – to access the public marketplace for funding. The most common reason companies choose to "go public" is that money raised through an IPO does not have to be repaid.

To pursue a traditional IPO, a company must first hire an investment bank. The investment bank facilitates the sale of the company's shares to the public. The investment bank's attorneys address the legal, SEC, and accounting issues surrounding an IPO. Investment banks prepare the offering prospectus, ensure the company's financials are properly audited, and generally shepherd the company through the entire IPO process. In addition, the investment bank will underwrite the offering.

In the last few months preceding the IPO, the investment bank puts on a road show to generate and gauge interest in the purchase of shares in the company. In the road show the company and its bankers present the case for investment in the company's shares including the industry, market, competition, and the company's place within all of that. The investment bank will value the company and come up with a range of price per share that the company should be priced at. The investment bank and its bankers will set the final subscription price towards the low end or high end of the range depending on the interest level of the institutions and wealthy individuals to whom the offering is presented.

The term *subscription* refers to the commitment to purchase multiplied by the number of shares all of the interested parties confirm they will buy. When assuming the company adhered to all the SEC rules and regulation regarding registration as a public company and fulfilled all the requirements, the investment bank finalizes the commitments. The company then goes public on the designated stock exchange: the American Stock Exchange (AMEX); the National Association of Securities and Dealers Automated Quotes (NASDAQ); and the New York Stock (NYSE).

Companies pursue IPOs for three primary reasons, as follows:

1. Raise money for expansion (facilities, equipment, personnel, etc.), debt retirement, and working capital;
2. Increase the shareholder's equity, thus strengthening the balance sheet. This expands the company's borrowing capacity, enabling it to obtain better credit terms and conditions; and
3. Create a liquid market for the owners' (venture capitalists, angels, founders, employees) stock.

A company should pursue an IPO when it primarily needs money for expansion. This means that the company is in sound financial condition and will not collapse or experience financial distress without the IPO funds. Just as other industries have cycles, so does the IPO market. In the best case scenario, the stock market would be at or near its height in receptivity to IPOs. When the market is receptive, institutional investors typically oversubscribe to the IPOs of strong companies resulting in large stock price jumps once the stock appears on the applicable stock exchange such as Nasdaq. Oversubscribe means investors commit to purchase more than the available shares of the company immediately before the shares debut on the stock exchange. When institutional investors (the primary purchasers) perceive IPOs more favorably, the company is valued higher. If the company has not been steadily preparing for an IPO, the IPO may take a year or more to bring to fruition.

Another way to go public – and one that more and more small companies with significant cash needs are pursuing – is through PIPEs and hedge funds, discussed above.

*(Another means of going public is through a reverse merger. However, since companies that utilize this method typically end up far below any investor's radar, this method will not be discussed in detail here. Many companies that go public through reverse mergers end up on the pink sheets – a financial wasteland where small companies that do not comply with SEC reporting requirements remain. These companies, usually listed on the OTC board, end up de-listed in one to three years.)*

This is by no means meant to provide a full description of the process a business takes to go public. It is simply meant to provide a basic understanding of how this option varies from other options of raising capital **and** to communicate the different options available to go public. If you are interested in pursuing an IPO as an exit strategy – now or in the future – consult with a reputable investment banker. If you have already procured funds from venture capitalists, consult with them as IPOs are still one of their preferred exit strategies, albeit one whose use oscillates with market receptivity.

Be aware that if your company revenues exceed $20 million, it must fully comply with Sarbanes-Oxley requirements. The Sarbanes-Oxley Act of 2002 is a federal law passed in response to the corporate scandals of Enron, WorldCom, Tyco International and others. The wide-ranging act set new standards for compliance for public company management, board of directors, and public accounting firms. In addition, as a public company, your company will be subject to much higher scrutiny and more external pressure. Your company's senior management will experience pressure to achieve short-term objectives, sometimes at the expense of long-term objectives.

**When to use IPOs.** If the following apply to your company, then you should strongly consider an IPO:

1. You believe your company has significant growth potential (i.e., could grow to $100 million or more in revenue in the next several years).
2. Your company has huge cash requirements to fuel the expansion.
3. Your company does not qualify for large bond, note or other debt financing, or will not generate the cash to service the debt.

▸ *Example Twenty-One: IPO financing.* When Excel Partners, a venture capital firm, invested in Douglas Technology, it did not seek a high, steady income stream from its investment. It invested with the expectation that Douglas would grow rapidly thus increasing the net worth of the company. Douglas would then "go public" allowing Excel the opportunity to reap most of its gain on investment.

By 2004, Douglas had grown so much that it required substantial capital to meet demand for its products both nationally and internationally. Douglas and its venture capital investors decided it was time for an initial public offering of stock. Going public would also allow Excel to sell some of its existing shares in Douglas to raise cash for other investments.

Douglas selected an underwriter, Silverman & Green, which specialized in technology companies as the lead underwriter. Because Douglas expected to raise $100 Million with its IPO, they expected Silverman & Green to form and manage a syndicate of underwriters of varying size to buy and resell the issue.

In tandem with Silverman & Green, outside lawyers and accountants, Douglas prepared a registration statement that included a prospectus, which it submitted to the SEC. After some back and forth, Douglas filed an amended statement with the SEC. Douglas then issued the final prospectus with the final offering price which had been established by Silverman & Green and the other underwriters during the road show. Douglas, per SEC requirements, mailed this prospectus to all prospective purchasers.

On September 5, 2004, Douglas went public at $55 per share. The underwriters began calling the buyers who had previously announced intentions of purchasing. The issue met expectations and all of the underwriters sold all of their Douglas stock at the issue price. By the end of the month, the shares were trading at $70. With the IPO, Douglas had successfully raised $110 million (2,000,000 shares sold at $55 per share).

**Private equity funds**. According to the Private Equity Growth Council, a Washington, D.C. research organization and resource center, in 2013 there were 2,797 private equity firms in the United States, a significant increase since 2000. The increase in private equity firms and funds is largely due to the bursting of the tech bubble in late 2000, the bursting of the housing and mortgage-backed security market in 2008 and the associated shift by individuals from the stock market into other forms of investment. In addition, the stock market run-up and the positive economic environment in the U.S. in the early 2000s led to a sizable increase in the ranks of high net worth individuals who qualified as accredited investors, although that number dropped during the latter part of the same decade.

Private equity firms and funds typically help companies make acquisitions, fund joint ventures, or otherwise fund expansion needs. Private equity firms enable business owners to pull cash out of the business to use for the following purposes: buy out a partner or partners; reinvest the proceeds into the business; or invest the proceeds into real estate or other investment vehicles to diversify the owner's portfolio.

Private equity firms typically expect annual returns of 20 to 35% with an exit, usually through a sale to a strategic or financial buyer, within three to seven years. Some private equity firms will allow a recapitalization through debt leverage as an exit strategy), if the company has the strong cash flows to enable this. In this scenario, a recapitalization enables the company's founder to buyout the private equity firm's stake Other PE firms will allow the sale of the firm's stake to a strategic investor or partner. Alternative exit strategies still must generate the 20 to 35% expected returns.

Some PE firms have lowered their expected annual returns for some industries for companies with certain characteristics to as low as 18% due to competition from venture capital funds and other private equity firms.

Once a private equity investor executes the Term Sheet or Letter of Commitment, the deal enters the negotiation and due diligence stage. Once this stage is reached, deals typically take 60 to 90 days on the low end up to 12 months on the high end to close. As previously mentioned in this book, a well-thought out Private Placement Memorandum (PPM) or similar document prepared in advance by the company's owner(s) can greatly shorten the negotiation stage.

Private equity firms typically charge 1-3% or more for legal and accounting fees. These fees increase with the complexity of the transaction. If you utilize the services of an investment banking advisor to access private equity funds, expect to pay an additional 1- 2% in fees.

The average private equity firm participates less in the management of a company than the average venture capital firm. The companies they deal with have already met or surpassed significant revenue hurdles, have a good plan for achieving additional growth, and have a strong management team. PE firms do not wish to "rock the boat" and interfere with a well-run operation. To monitor their investments, PE firms typically take a seat on the board and participate in all board meetings, mandate a say in all strategic shifts and decisions, and review quarterly financial statements and monthly financial reports.

***When to use private equity funds.*** If your company has revenues of at least $10 million, growth projections in either income or revenue that equate to 20 to 35% annual returns on equity, you need capital to expand organically (expand through sales and marketing), or you need capital to purchase another company or companies as part of an acquisition strategy, these conditions may justify turning to private equity for capital. If your business is growing rapidly but your business partner or other investors want out, private equity is a great capital source to buy out your business partners or investors. In the latter case, the equity infusion would be called a recapitalization because you are ***replacing*** capital from one source with another (i.e., restructuring your balance sheet), not adding capital.

***Resources.*** The National Association of Investment Companies (NAIC) – provides articles, research, and links to various private equity firms at http://www.naicvc.com. An appropriately named website, Private Equity provides a list of over 1,300 private equity firms with links to their respective websites at http://privateequity.com.

➡ ***Example Twenty-Two: Private equity fund financing.*** BannerWorld, a small promotions company based in Delaware, was founded by two people with complementary skill sets. The company reached sales of $15 million by the end of fiscal year 2005. Lou, one of the founders, had encountered a series of health problems that led to a decision to leave the business earlier than he had planned. Because both founders played active roles in the company, and Lou needed funds to support his early separation from the business, Lou and Mark, the co-founder, determined that a sale of Lou's stake was the best option.

However, Mark did not have the funds to buy out Lou's 45% stake and the company could not handle the debt load required to generate the funds to buy out the stake. After much consideration, the two decided that a private equity firm was the best option. Mark believed that the right private equity firm would also help him find Lou's management replacement.

BannerWorld successfully engaged two private equity firms to raise $6.2 million. The two firms took a combined 35% stake in the company. The private equity firms used a combination of debt and equity to provide the company with the capital needed to buy Lou out. Mark used much of the remaining proceeds to hire additional staff and purchase equipment. The one private equity firm that contributed the bulk of the equity proceeds retained a board seat and advised Mark on his successful entry into the specialty advertising market. Garnering sufficient capital to operate and grow the business and obtaining a strategic advisor alleviated the vast majority of Mark's concerns about BannerWorld's continued viability. The capital infusion also helped Mark's own personal financial situation, providing Mark with the wherewithal – financial, emotional, and mental – to focus wholly on running the business.

➠ *Example Twenty-Three: Bank and Private equity fund financing.* Evans Family Foods formed as a company for the express purpose of acquiring small food manufacturing companies. The owner, an investor, hired an investment banking advisor to assist with the search and the financing. The advisor located a sausage manufacturing company outside of Durham, North Carolina whose owners wanted to sell due to a pronounced partnership disagreement.

The advisor and the Evans' owner negotiated a $4.5 million purchase price, then lined up bank financing for $3.25 million. The investor-owner contributed $250,000 of his own money. The advisor solicited the small private equity funds he knew to generate the financing to cover the $1 million equity gap. The private equity funds agreed to provide $2 million in financing with $1 million for equity and $1 million in subordinated debt. Anything less and they refused to do the deal. Evan's owner-investor and his advisor subsequently reduced the bank's term loan amount to $2.25 million, which enabled the PE firms to fund $1 million each.

**Private placements.** Private placement refers to sale of a relatively small number of shares in your company directly to institutional investors such as insurance companies, pension funds, banks, mutual funds, and foundations. Individuals classified as accredited investors also may invest in a private placement. Securities and Exchange Commission (SEC) registration is not required for the shares as long as the securities are bought and held for investment purposes and not for resale. The company discloses the details of the business much like in a business plan but also provides in-depth information regarding the investment and its risks in the Private Placement Memorandum (PPM). Both publicly and privately held companies can and do utilize private placements.

Private placements offer an attractive alternative for small businesses to obtain equity funding. They provide a high degree of flexibility. Institutions, defined as entities in the business of holding assets, have a longer time horizon than venture capitalists and angels – five to ten years – and are therefore more patient. Institutions include banks, pension funds, mutual funds, investment companies, and insurance companies. Furthermore, institutions often seek 10 to 20% returns versus 20 to 30% returns. In addition, the costs are much lower than pursuing venture capitalists or private equity firms or selling via an IPO or secondary public offering, and the process is much faster. Moreover, the investors are generally not interested in obtaining control of the company. They usually do not even want board seats. Finally, private placements can provide a quicker way to raise money than through the usual venture capital path.

To utilize this form of financing, you will need a thorough, viable business plan and a private placement memorandum disclosing all the facts regarding the business and the investment including the risks inherent in the investment. You will use the business plan to craft portions of the PPM that discuss the business, its industry, markets, and competitors. You will need to engage the services of a lawyer or law firm that has experience in private placements to assist in crafting the PPM. Law firms and investment banking entities with lawyers on staff charge $5,000 to $10,000 and up for a PPM, depending on the size and complexity of the business and offering. There are business advisors and consultants that serve growing firms that keep templates of PPMs and modify them accordingly for their clients. Because they use existing templates as a base, they typically charge a significantly reduced fee of $2,000 to $4,000 for their services. You can then have your attorney review the documents and recommend changes for a few hundred dollars.

Historically, annual returns in the private market are higher than the historical returns for the public stock exchanges. Consequently, the private investor market presents an attractive alternative for small business owners and investors. Private placement offers a viable way for growing companies to tap into the private investment pool of capital to obtain business financing. Private placement has fewer limitations and constraints and requires minimal ceding of control compared to that which occurs often with venture capital firms, going public and, to a lesser extent, with private equity firms.

***When to use private placements.*** If you are a small business in the third stage – after start-up and the first or second round of financing-- and you seek expansion or growth funding. This is ***not*** to be confused with angel financing.

***Resources.*** To learn more about private placements, refer to the following websites: www.privateequityonline.com, www.privateraise.com, and www.fundingpost.com.

⏵***Example Twenty-Four: Private placements.*** Avery White, a graduate of a top-tier business school, eschewed the permanent employment route at investment banks, consulting firms, and corporations that most of his peers pursued. Instead, having obtained his MBA in Entrepreneurial Management, he opted to immediately put his knowledge to work by starting his own vitamin distribution company, ABC Vitamin Company. Fortunately for Avery, he was married to another business school graduate who agreed to pay all personal and some business expenses while he pursued his dream of starting and building a company.

Avery completed his business plan, sourced manufacturers, built a website, and began work on a catalog. Then he realized he would need access to a greater source of capital – from his calculations, ~$250,000. He would keep his costs down by direct sourcing the products from the manufacturers, but he still needed capital to build out ABC Vitamin, market, and staff the company for a national and international roll-out.

Since ABC's revenues were in a nascent stage, Avery knew he would not qualify for debt financing nor could his firm service the debt at that stage. After some thought, Avery decided to tap his network of former business school classmates, professors, and others to raise funds. To do this, he obtained an IPO prospectus from one of his investment banking friends and used it as the template to create a PPM.

Avery then hired an attorney to review the PPM. After incorporating the recommended changes, Avery began actively soliciting everyone he could think of. In four months he raised $220,000, just shy of the $250,000 he sought.

**Venture capital.** According to the National Venture Capital Association's 2013 Yearbook, in 2012 venture capitalists (VCs) pumped $26.7 billion into more than 3,000 firms. Only 15.4% of venture financing were initial investments. In addition, 33% of the $26.7 billion was invested in start-up and early stage companies in 2012, versus 19% in 2005. In addition, 22.4% of the total went to finance later stage companies. This points to a continued risk averseness of VC firms to early stage companies. Some venture firms are now nearly in direct competition with some private equity firms since switching their concentration to funding late stage companies who they now deem as much more likely to realize an equity event such as an acquisition within the ensuing three to five years.

Venture capital firms still have large pools of funds to employ. Some firms are still sitting on non-performing assets (companies) that they have not yet spun out of their respective portfolios. Some firms have been reticent about doing so. The losses are only on paper until the company is actually dissolved or sold at a significant loss. Venture capital firms, more than ever, want management teams with direct business and industry experience, large market opportunities, and sizable revenues with profitability within sight range.

The bulk of the venture capital firms are based in Silicon Valley, California. Other regional markets with a sizable venture capitalist presence include the Boston, Massachusetts area and the New York City area. Most venture capital firms refuse to be the sole venture capitalist investing in an enterprise. Thus two to three firms at a time typically invest in one company. If you need $10 million, two firms will invest $5 million each or three firms will invest $3.3 Million each, or a similar agreed-upon split. This validates their respective projections and spreads the risk.

***When to use venture capital.*** When you need a minimum of $3 to $5 million in capital to expand your technology-based business and anticipate a need for additional capital infusions in the ensuing three to five years, you may consider VC firms. "Technology-based" includes information technology, medical/health/life sciences, and Internet. Other segments of interest to venture capitalists include energy, especially renewable energy, media and entertainment, and consumer products. When your company is producing revenue, has a strong management team, and is well-positioned to exploit the market, consider venture capital. This would be especially true when you eventually want to go public or be acquired by a large company in your industry.

***Resources.*** The *National Venture Capital Association* has industry news and links to various private equity financing sources available at www.nvca .org. The *Venture Capital Resource Directory* offers a complete listing of active venture capital firms in the U.S. from A to Z. The directory with contact information for each firm is available by download, CD-Rom, or book for a fee, available at http://www.vfinance.com/home.asp?Toolpage=vencaentire.asp. *VcPro Database* provides *a* global directory of VC funds and firms accessible at www.vcaonline.com.

⏵ *Example: Twenty-Five: Venture capital financing.* Many examples of venture capital usage are fairly well-known. Google, Mindspring, Intel, Nortel Networks, Global Crossing, Genentech – all successfully utilized venture capital to obtain the capital needed to grow their businesses to tremendous size. Many lesser known companies in the same industries also successfully garnered and utilized venture capital. These industries include technology related industries such as telecommunications, bio-technology, and the medical field.

Therefore, this book does not contain any specific dedicated examples of venture capital usage. Refer to the resources and websites listed above.

PART III:

# DEBT & EQUITY FINANCING SOURCES:
Blended/Hybrid Capital

# CHAPTER 10

# Hybrid Capital and Non-Traditional Sources – Overview

For many small and mid-sized companies experiencing stable but slow growth, hybrid capital may provide the best funding choice. Why? Because many of these companies operate as lifestyle businesses for their owners. Alternatively, many owners of these businesses have taken the company as far as their skill set allows. Typically, the company needs to make operational and management changes to significantly increase its growth and value. These companies have enough consistent cash flow to pay off debt but may not have enough assets or cash flow to fully fund an acquisition or significant expansion with 100% debt.

Stable, slow growing companies also make attractive investment candidates but generally have valuations too low for the existing owners to agree to outright equity investment or purchase at the lower valuation. In these cases, hybrid options provide the best of both the debt and equity worlds. Hybrid options offer a higher debt load than a company could qualify for with traditional lenders solely on collateral and cash flow. Hybrid options also offer equity conversion rights that enable hybrid capital providers to participate in the upside as the company restructures, revamps or vastly expands its operations and consequently increases its overall valuation.

According to Investopedia, hybrid capital "combines two or more different financial instruments" generally with "both debt and equity characteristics." The Financial Times provides another definition for hybrid capital. "Hybrid capital is a form of debt that has been substituted for equity. This type of debt has both debt and equity features. This covers a variety of instruments, such as preference shares, that are not pure equity but have traditionally been deemed close enough." Examples of hybrid capital include convertible debt securities including bonds, which larger companies may use; debt with warrants attached debt with mandatory conversion provisions; and promissory notes with conversion options to common stock. Preferred stock, which is equity with debt-like characteristics is another example of hybrid capital, especially those with conversion options to common stock.

Hybrid capital lies on the debt-equity continuum, which type its closest to depends on the specifics of the hybrid capital used and the terms of the associated agreement. Actually, over hybrid capital's life, the characteristics may change and swing from being more equity-like to more debt-like and vice versa. Companies use hybrid capital to access a lower cost of capital than equity but with many of the same benefits. Debt typically has the lowest cost of capital and hybrid capital allows you to tap into that lower cost debt at a level that suits your company and situation.

Companies also find hybrid capital attractive because it allows them to access equity-like capital without the dilution that equity brings. Dilution refers to the decrease in your percentage of ownership. For example, you own 70% of your company's 100,000 outstanding shares. That means you own 70,000 shares. If you issue another 10,000 shares to sell to investors, your ownership percentage changes to 70,000 divided by 110,000 shares or 63.64%. By issuing more equity, you diluted --or reduced--your equity from 70% to 63.64%.

If you have a growing company that needs capital but does not qualify for sufficient bank loans, preferred stock with conversion rights can be your answer. This type of preferred stock provides you with access to equity capital without dilution. With large corporations, most preferred stock comes without voting rights, which lessens the direct interference of investors with the way you run and manage your business. However, most smaller firms that bring in venture capitalists issue preferred stock which gives the venture capitalists voting rights. Although preferred stock typically requires dividend payments, you can structure those dividend payments to only accumulate. The payout would occur before any distributions were made to common shareholders when your company returns to or reaches a better cash position.

Beyond hybrid capital, creative financing sources present additional venues for you to obtain the capital or resources you need to grow your business. Small business owners approach the money they need for the businesses a number of ways. Unfortunately, too many just think of credit cards, bank loans, and venture capital. Of course, most know they'd never qualify for the latter but they think about it! I say "unfortunately" because believing you have a number of options is the first step in identifying those options and finding the money you need to help establish and grow your business. This includes obtaining strong management to complement and supplement the owner's skills and abilities.

Entrepreneurs and business owners can access non-traditional funding sources by taking the same creative approach with financing that they often use when addressing issues in other parts of their business. For example, a company with minimal available funds determines that an effective marketing and public relations campaign could drastically grow its business. Instead of pursuing funding for this campaign the company could use guerilla marketing and public relations tactics to vaunt its exposure to and standing among its target audience. Guerilla marketing requires a highly creative approach and a concentrated effort. Take this same perspective with financing your business and you will reap similar results.

To get creative, you must focus on what you need the money for, not the actual money. This is why investors always want to see sources and uses of funds. They want to know how you will spend the funds they invest, to determine if they think the uses you have in mind are compatible with their visions for how funds should be used. Write down the amount of funds you need and each item you need them for. For example: Employ a general manager - $100,000; Marketing campaign to increase exposure to target customers - $50,000; Deferred maintenance on office and production area - $150,000; Software - $15,000. Next, begin to brainstorm ways to get what you need and want. Again, do not focus on the money, but on the ways you could cover the items you need.

Continuing with creatively brainstorming your financing needs, ask yourself, "How do I get my marketing needs covered?" instead of "How do I get the $50,000 I need for my marketing campaign?" The use of creative financing requires you to get really clear about why you need money and what specifically, in detail, you will do with that money. As you go through your list of needs, following are some creative questions that come to mind which could lead you to solutions.

Do I need a full-time general manager or can I use an interim GM/COO type and split the cost with another firm? Is my company in a position to offer equity or profit-sharing to a GM candidate to reduce the upfront salary needs? Do I have the skill set to launch a guerilla marketing campaign at a substantially reduced cost? Do I need marketing or public relations and, if the latter, how could I do this effectively without hiring a costly PR firm? Have I identified the most effective marketing I can do or will I just throw money at different marketing opportunities and see what sticks? Is there an entity out there I could share our office or warehouse space with who would handle the maintenance? Can I barter with a maintenance firm to provide them with something they need in return for maintenance work? Are there software as a service, or SaaS, applications which allow my company access to its capabilities for a monthly fee instead of an upfront investment? Are any companies offering specials, discounts, grants or test usage for the type of software we need? Can I get access to the software through a partnership?

Thinking and asking questions like this will help you find the capital you need faster. When you remain open to the possibilities, your mind --or someone else's --will always identify the solution that works well for you. You also increase the likelihood that you will receive a call from or meet someone who has exactly what you seek.

# CHAPTER 11

# Hybrid Capital Sources

Many people invest in stocks and bonds through brokerage firms. Years ago all brokerage firms had offices but now some discount brokerage firms only have an online presence.

**Brokerage accounts and brokerage firms.** Most brokerage firms now allow individuals to leverage their brokerage accounts to secure a line of credit. Stated another way, the accounts serve as collateral for the line of credit. Many firms require a stated minimum value, often as high as $750,000, when using the line of credit to purchase anything besides stock, options, or mutual funds – or anything else that the brokerage directly offers for sale to its clients. This minimum must be comprised of blue chip stocks and mutual funds – securities with minimal volatility. Brokerage firms allowing this include UBS, Morgan Stanley, and JP Morgan Chase. Numerous other smaller entities likely offer something similar, sometimes at lower stated minimums. To confirm, check with your brokerage firm.

***When to use brokerage accounts.*** If you have a large brokerage account but do not wish to liquidate the assets to fund the start-up, purchase, or growth of your business, leveraging your brokerage account presents a highly viable alternative.

*Reputable sources of brokerage debt and information regarding leverage.* This list includes JP Morgan Chase, Goldman Sachs, TD Waterhouse, Prudential, Merrill Lynch, Charles Schwab, UBS, and may include other investment banks and brokerage firms.

➤ *Example Twenty-Six: Equipment financing and brokerage accounts.* Terry needed approximately $1 million to purchase equipment, lease warehouse and office space, hire additional staff, and execute the orders her relatively young company had just received. Terry did not have strong banking relationships, nor did she have significant personal net worth to fund her business expansion needs. Terry spoke to a friend of hers whom she considered business savvy. This friend had taken an early retirement buyout offer and had recently sold his home in a nice California suburb. She told him she needed funds to expand her business but, beyond a bank, she didn't know where to start.

Her friend, Michael, listened intently to Terry's description of her business and her issues. He asked a number of pointed questions. He then told her he held a significant amount of liquid assets in his brokerage account and had once margined those funds to fund the down payment on a previous house. Since he held most of his portfolio in blue chip and relatively stable companies, he thought he may be able to margin his account again. Michael asked Terry to compile further documentation for him and said he would follow up with his brokerage firm.

Michael later told Terry he could provide the full $1 million in financing using a credit line tied to his brokerage account. However, he thought she should be a little more creative and aggressive, and pursue equipment financing for the equipment, utilize contractors or outside firms for most of her non-critical personnel needs, and negotiate a staggered lease with an option to buy. All of this would reduce her immediate and near-term cash needs and his need to immediately tap into the $1 Million credit line.

Terry used Michael's funding commitment and her business plan to negotiate an advantageous lease and procure equipment financing. By outsourcing her sales and marketing and using an employment staffing agency for several of her other positions, she successfully cut her anticipated personnel overhead in half. In the end, Michael only pulled out $300,000 from his brokerage credit line to support Terry.

Michael has since joined Terry's advisory board. He continues to support her and her company as it expands. Terry continues to use Michael's financing commitment to negotiate better terms with suppliers, contractors, and others. Michael also convinced her to switch to a smaller community bank with whom she is now building a strong relationship.

**Insurance companies.** Insurance companies participate often in real-estate backed agreements, less often in pure business financing. In addition, insurance companies rarely provide, business financing to firms with minimal high grade assets. However, insurance companies do participate in private placements, often structuring their involvement as an equity or profit participation deal. They charge a lower interest rate but also take a portion of the profits over the term of the loan.

***When to use insurance companies.*** If you are a real estate developer or purchaser, especially if you focus on commercial or industrial properties, and you have a track record, insurance companies can provide the financing your company needs. If you are working on your first development project, insurance companies may be interested in providing the take-out financing.

## Mezzanine finance.

Mezzanine finance providers and mezzanine funds package equity and debt in a myriad of combinations to purchase a business, fund an acquisition or merger, finance large expansion initiatives, or retire existing debt. Essentially, mezzanine financing is debt with warrants attached.

A warrant enables the owner of the warrant to buy a specific number of company shares at some point in the future at a specified price. When tied to debt, a warrant gives the debt holder the potential to participate in the upside should a corporation's stock increase in value. Warrants are rights that allow conversion to an equity interest in a company at a pre-determined conversion factor, often if certain terms are not met. For example, for every $10,000 in loan proceeds, the company can purchase x shares at y price. Phrased another way, warrants make mezzanine financing debt with an "equity kicker."

For example, your corporation wants to raise $2 million from an investor to acquire a competitor. You prefer to use debt, but neither your company nor the competitor qualifies for a pure bank loan for that amount. An investment firm agrees to lend you $2 million at nine percent interest but with warrants attached. Those warrants, if exercised, enable the investor to buy up to 30% of your company's outstanding shares at $10 each up until four years after the loan closing date.

Mezzanine debt is generally subordinated to bank debt and other "senior" lenders such as venture finance companies. As a hybrid of debt and equity financing that generally includes subordinated convertible debt and preferred stock, with warrants or options attached, mezzanine financing is generally not collateralized by a company's assets. Mezzanine financing is often treated as *equity* on a company's balance sheet.

Mezzanine capital resides between senior debt and equity. It typically is issued in the following forms: subordinated debt; preferred stock; equity provided by a warrant, conversion feature, or purchase rights to common stock (options). Not meeting loan repayment terms triggers a default which triggers these conversion features. Mezzanine financing providers serve as both lenders and shareholders incorporating safety of principal and equity appreciation.

Venture companies and alternative lending entities seeking rates of return of 20-30% usually provide mezzanine financing. Small Business Investment Corporations (SBICs) provide mezzanine financing. These entities were created by an act of Congress and are regulated by the SBA. A moratorium on fund creation was placed on SBICs in 2003 due to poor performance but that moratorium was lifted. However, beware. Do not use the SBA list of SBICs. I personally called and spoke with the CFO or investment representative of 5 companies on the list and only one was actively investing. The other four had morphed into different entities but were still licensed as SBICs because they still held investments in one or two companies. Instead, use the information provided by the National Association of Investment Companies and the Small Business Investor Alliance, both of which focus on funds that are currently investing.

If you want mezzanine financing, you will need the following: an industry track record with a reputable product or service; a history of profitability or, at least, breakeven performance; and a written, strategically sound plan to expand the business. These criteria are the same as that for companies seeking private equity. Therefore, companies that qualify for mezzanine financing often qualify for private equity.

In addition, mezzanine financing is also considered bridge financing for new but profitable companies that do not have the collateral or track record to qualify for bank loans and credit lines. "Bridge" financing refers to the financing's purpose or ability to bridge the gaps in financing between equity infusion and bank qualification.

***When to use mezzanine financing.*** A rapidly growing young company with a strong and experienced management team that procured its second round of equity funding but that is not yet ready for an IPO is a great candidate for mezzanine financing. High quality, established middle market companies with a record of generating consistently strong earnings and cash flow should strongly consider mezzanine financing. If that company also has well-defined operation and expansion strategies, yet is unable to obtain adequate financing from its lender, and prefers to minimize the equity dilution of the current owners, mezzanine financing provides an excellent financing option.

- If you are part of a management team considering a management buyout or considering purchasing a stable but growing company with good cash flow via a leveraged buyout, mezzanine financing may be an excellent option.

- If you have viable strategic and operational plans to grow your company significantly through acquisitions or organically through joint ventures, partnerships, and similar means, mezzanine financing can provide the expansion financing needed.

- If you need to re-capitalize the firm in order to buy out a partner or other investor, or you need to divest a division, mezzanine financing can provide the necessary funds to accomplish these objectives.

Compared to the typical equity injection, the "lender" typically subjects the "borrower" of mezzanine financing to minimal due diligence. Therefore, if speed is a concern (for example, you have a looming deadline to close on an acquisition), and your company fits the profiles above, mezzanine financing is again an excellent option.

⮕ *Example Twenty-Seven: Direct lender/CDC/Mezzanine financing.* Damon Darrell entered into negotiations with a partner to buy a food distribution company with $11.8 million in annual revenue. This distribution company was well-managed, with great cash flow and profit margins, and was located in a section of the metro area convenient to transportation providers. Damon and his partner signed a Letter of Intent to buy the company for $6.5 million, which included $2.5 million for the land and building the company occupied.

Damon approached a direct lender about financing a portion of the acquisition. The direct lender informed Damon that she could likely only finance up to $3 million of the loan. However, as the acquisition included real estate which was located inside a certain geographical area, she thought she could team with a community development corporation to finance a total of $5 million. She contacted the CDC and all three entities met to discuss the pending transaction. The CDC confirmed its interest and agreed to co-finance the $5 million loan – $2 million from the CDC, or 40% of the loan amount, and $3 million from the direct lender, or 60% of the loan amount – using an SBA-guaranteed loan.

Damon still had to come up with $1.5 Million in financing. He considered venture merchant bank financing but, upon further investigation, determined that the direct lender and CDC would place a blanket lien on all the receivables and inventory, nullifying the collateral source for the venture bank. Now that he had $5 million in senior, fully collateralized loans, Damon pursued subordinated, unsecured debt. He approached the owners and requested owner financing. However, even after much negotiation and repeatedly stressing the lower tax impact and additional revenue in retirement, the owners refused to provide financing.

Damon contacted a mergers and acquisition (M&A) advisor he had met earlier. They discussed Damon's situation. The advisor strongly recommended that Damon pursue mezzanine financing since the cash flows would support it. This would enable Damon and his partner to retain a much higher ownership stake than if they pursued private equity financing or angel investors. Damon agreed. The advisor recommended that they tie up the target company's current COO in an employment contract and give him 5% equity in the company because mezzanine funds like to see management buyouts or some portion of the management team remain on board. Damon did so.

The M&A advisor secured $1 million in funding from a mezzanine fund. The fund wanted an annualized 18% return, so they structured the proceeds as a five-year note with a 10% coupon, with the remaining 8% expected to come from exercising the attached warrants. The warrants were structured to provide a conversion value of $400,000 at the end of five years. Given the anticipated $15 million value of the company in five years, the $400,000 in warrants would equate to an equity position of 2.67% at that time. (A default on payments due on the note by the company would trigger additional warrants to the mezzanine firm and a resulting greater stake in the company.)

Damon and his partner had sizable brokerage accounts with investments largely in mutual funds and blue chip stocks. Thus, they explored the option of converting their respective accounts to margin accounts instead of liquidating the proceeds. After converting to a margin account, they extracted a total of $300,000 through lines of credit drawn against their portfolios. A business acquaintance of theirs agreed to inject the remaining $200,000 in required equity.

Damon and his partner realized that they had not put any money aside for working capital. They determined that the company's customers typically paid in 30 days and that the cash flow gap between payables and receivables rarely exceeded $95,000. They subsequently approached the direct lender for a $100,000 working capital line of credit. After looking over the numbers and the financing package, the direct lender agreed to include a $150,000 line of credit as part of its overall financing package.

**Raising funds through acquisitions.** Firms may combine to enhance their fund-raising ability when a "cash-rich" firm merges with or acquires a "cash poor" firm.

Banks and other lenders look at the historical operations of the respective firms and the projected results to assess the likelihood of continued operations and the ability of the combined firm to service the debt provided. Therefore, if your firm is "cash poor," but you acquire a "cash rich" firm, your combined company's overall ability to service debt increases tremendously, resulting in the combined firm qualifying for larger loans. If the firm you acquire actually holds a lot of cash in marketable securities and other readily convertible sources, you now have that cash to use for additional expansion.

Sometimes cash rich companies are so because they operate in low growth markets with high margins. A merger with your company may be attractive to the owner of the cash rich company because, although your firm has limited cash flow, it has superior expansion and growth potential. Your firm's rapid growth is likely the reason for its limited cash.

## CHAPTER 12

# Non-Traditional Capital Sources

C o-branding. Co-branding occurs when two or more companies combine their marketing efforts to reach customers in the same target market. Some examples of co-branding efforts include Dairy Queen's use of the Butterfinger and HeathBar for Blizzards or an American Airline Visa. An example involving three companies is the GE-branded water heater offered exclusively by Home Depot but manufactured by a non-GE-related firm in France.

**Cooperative (co-op).** According to dictionary.com, a cooperative is a "jointly owned enterprise engaging in the  production or distribution of goods or the supplying of services, operated by its members for their mutual benefit, typically organized" by an affinity group. Asian, Arab, and North African immigrants most often employ the co-op model for various types of businesses. This model typically requires more sacrifice in the early years and an innate trust level for the co-op leader. Most native-born Americans will not commit to the years of sacrifice nor trust in their "neighbors" in the way many immigrants do.

Native-born Americans most often employ the co-op model to form utility co-ops and agriculture co-ops to harness their collective buying power. In this way, members reap immediate benefits. Members all pay monthly or annual dues to operate the co-op. The co-ops often sell to non-members but at higher prices.

**Crowdfunding.** Crowdfunding engages those who "donate" to your business. Crowdfunding provides you with access to a community of donors who fund your business without the usual hassle involved with identifying, pursuing and engaging angel investments. A company needing to raise several thousand to several hundred thousand can launch a campaign on a crowdfunding site to raise money. You can set up the account in the name of your business, campaign and convince others to donate to your business.

Under the federal JOBS Act, the federal government enacted new rules to allow companies to "equity" crowdfund with accredited investors. Later rules, due in 2014, will enable non-accredited investors to invest small amounts into your company. Read the section on equity crowdfunding for a detailed discussion.

Under donation crowdfunding, you specify how much you need, what you will use the funds for and how long your campaign will last. You create and launch a campaign which, for the companies that are the most successful at attracting donations, includes a compelling write-up, a reason, and an engaging video. Some providers allow you to fund anything – the entire business, a specific project or product launch. Others solely fund specific projects. If you do not meet your funding target, most crowdfunding sites either assess your fee at a higher percentage of the total proceeds or never fund your campaign and dismiss it entirely. You must read the instructions and guidelines thoroughly for each crowdfunding entity you consider in order to select the provider that best fits your company's needs and its communication and marketing capabilities.

Because crowdfunding, as currently structured, connects "donors" to companies, these donors will not see a return on their investment as an investor would. You will not need to keep them apprised of the progress of your business nor provide them with distributions once your company becomes profitable and cash flow positive. What you offer are gifts or rewards. This can include discounts, freebies or your product or service when it becomes available. It can also include promotional products such as pens, t-shirts or hats or a listing in a book or on your website.

Offer different items at different donation price points to encourage larger amounts. Be creative. For suggestions check out what current and former successful campaigns offered. Ask your business partners, employees, associates and friends for suggestions. Several companies have raised hundreds of thousands more than anticipated. However, the average funding size ranges from $3,700 to $5,000 due to the high number of projects which fail to fund, depending on the site. This includes businesses, creative projects, and non-profits. However, in 2012 17 projects attracted over $1 million in funding. How compelling and engaging your write-up, videos, and giveaways are will be the primary drivers of your success.

▶ *Example Twenty-Eight: Crowdfunding.* Hundreds of small businesses have raised money through crowdfunding. One athletic products start-up with a new work-out tracking device raised $400,000 from a donation campaign it launched on a popular crowdfunding site. Its original goal was $40,000 but its campaign went viral, attracting the attention of many others around the world. In addition to other giveaways, the company mentioned donors of a certain size on its website and pledged copies of its first products. In addition, non-traditional businesses have raised money for projects including musicians who raised capital to fund the cost of creating and distributing a CD, independent or amateur filmmakers who raised capital to fund a movie project, and authors who raised money to fund living expenses while they wrote.

**Resources.** Kickstarter and Indiegogo are two of the largest crowdfunding sites for for-profit enterprises or endeavors. See the Resources section for more information.

**Customer deposits or prepays.** If you have new customers, especially small business owners or self-employed individuals, you can request deposits on the product or service they purchase. Or, if you have established relationships because your company provides great products or service in a timely fashion, you can ask your customers to pre-pay. To avoid conveying the message that your firm is encountering financial difficulty or is finding it difficult to garner other sources of financing, offer a discount for pre-payment.

To the extent that you can decrease the amount of time between the delivery of your product or service and the receipt of payments for those products or services, you can increase the amount of operational cash flow available. To the extent that you can increase your operating margins and reduce your fixed and variable expenses, you increase the amount of cash from operations that is available to fund growth initiatives.

If you do not know what your break-even point is, or what your operating and profit margins are, enlist the services of a consultant, cost accountant, or coach immediately. You are likely losing a great deal of money! Contrary to popular belief, what you do not know absolutely can harm you. Ignorance is NOT bliss. In fact, ignorance can drive you into financial failure but knowledge — of your business financial and operational fundamentals – can save you.

**Employees.** Pay employees with options, restricted stock, or stock. Alternatively, pay employees solely on a commission basis. In the latter case, you do not pay the employee until she generates revenue. This reduces your company's upfront pay-outs until its cash becomes more certain.

Employees can also make loans to the company for specific purchases. The employee essentially serves as the lender instead of a bank, equipment lender, or other more typical financing source. If you use this option, structure a formal loan agreement to protect both parties – your business and your employee.

**Equity as Payment.** Pay consultants and service providers with equity via stock or options. To use this option successfully you must sell others on the viability of and growth prospects for your business. They must believe that they will reap at least what they would have had they been paid in cash.

➠ *Example Twenty-Nine: Equity as payment financing.* According to a Wall Street Journal article, the founders of Google used equity as payment wherever possible. At least two consultants worked on the business plan that Google used to obtain angel financing. Both were offered options. One demanded a $3,000 up-front payment. Two years after Google went public, the consultant who took the options had a stake in Google worth $7 Million.

**Franchising.** Franchising is a method of distributing and marketing products and services through a business format. A company needs capital to launch a franchising program and expansion capital to build it. However, the capital requirements for franchising pale when compared to the expansion capital needs of traditional growth avenues.

Companies choose to franchise for the following reasons:

1. Increase market penetration at a faster rate with lower cost;
2. Involve motivated owners instead of employees;
3. Push down responsibilities such as site selection, build-out, and hiring to owner-operators;
4. Better target consumers of service through coordinated marketing efforts;
5. Obtain efficiencies and scale; and

6.  Sell services and products into the distribution network.

Companies choosing this option will need to enlist the use of a highly capable franchise consultant and attorney. These individuals will help build out the offering, terms, and required financing. They will also help create the Uniform Franchise Offering Circular (UFOC), which all franchisors must make available to interested franchisees.

For more information, contact the International Franchise Association, www.franchise.org

■■▶ *Example Thirty: Franchise financing.* Food franchises such as McDonald's, Kentucky Fried Chicken, and, more recently, Moe's Southwest Grill adopted this expansion model early on. Other industries that utilize franchising business models for expansion include business coaching enterprises such as Action International, supplementary educational providers such as Sylvan Learning Centers, and automotive repair service providers such as MAACO and AAMCO.

**Grants.** The *Small Business Innovation Research* (SBIR) grant program is a federally funded program that offers approximately $2 billion annually to small businesses through 11 participating agencies including the National Institutes of Health and the Department of Defense. SBIR grants provide research and development funding and technical validation at a time when many small companies may have few options. SBIR grants are an excellent source of business capital for providers of innovative technology to a number of industries. The agencies dispense grants in two phases:

*Phase 1* is essentially a research feasibility study. Phase I provides up to $100,000 in grants to be spent over a duration of eight months. The application, review, and reward process takes three to six months for Phase I.

*Phase II* covers the commercialization process and provides up to $750,000 in grants to be spent over a duration of 24 months. Application to Phase II is only possible after successful completion of Phase I. The application, review, and reward process takes six to nine months. Various federal agencies sponsor SBIR grants.

The U.S. Department of Agriculture (USDA) offers subsidized loans and grants to companies operating in rural areas.

Otherwise, contrary to the late night television shows and e-mail spam marketing campaigns, there are almost **no** federal grants for businesses. The grants that do exist for businesses are usually state and local economic development grants and private foundation grants.

*Economic development grants* are often available in rural areas or in cities with designated economic development zones. The purpose of these grants is to stimulate the rural economy or blighted and depressed urban area by creating numerous jobs over a designated time frame and increasing the tax base of the county or city area. Thus, these grants are usually designated for and offered only to those businesses deemed likely to create 50 or more (sometimes 100 or more) jobs in rural areas, a smaller number in urban empowerment zones.

➥ *Example Thirty-One: Grants financing.* Complex Technology Seekers Inc. (CTS), a provider of global positioning-related mobile software solutions, first sought angel investment to complete the build out of their product demo and market to prospective clients. However, many of the angel investors balked at the company's minimal $110,000 revenue. The ones that expressed interest wanted to pay less per share than the company deemed appropriate.

The Chief Technology Officer of the company, Ted, heard about the SBIR grant. He asked one of his strategic advisors to investigate the program's applicability to CTS. When the advisor reported that CTS' product was a great fit and that the SBIR grant would pay to complete the product's development, create the demo, and create the product marketing plan, Ted decided to pursue the grant. Since Ted held a PhD in Mathematics, research and development were his first loves. He found a grant writer to help him draft the SBIR grant proposal.

CTS submitted the proposal and was subsequently awarded an SBIR Phase I grant for $105,000 five months later. Over the ensuing months CTS successfully complied with all the terms of the grant. CTS then submitted a proposal for Phase II of the SBIR grant and won. Phase II proceeds amounted to $500,000.

With the help of the SBIR grants and product development resources provided through a strategic partner, CTS sold its products and generated $1 million in revenue. CTS later solicited angel investors – this time to fund its sales and marketing efforts. The company raised over 85% of the funds it needed to accomplish its three-year objectives.

**Insurance.** To generate cash, you can borrow against the cash value of your personal whole life, universal life or similar cash value life insurance policy. Term life insurance has no cash value, and thus is not available as a source of funds.

**Licensing.** Licensing involves selling the rights to manufacture or distribute your company's product, selling the rights to provide your firm's services, or selling the rights to your company's name. The licensing agreement can be short-term, long-term, specific to a geographic region, or use-specific. The options and combinations are nearly limitless. You should structure the agreement to meet the needs and address the concerns of the parties to the agreement.

Major sports leagues such as the NBA or NFL license the use of their logos to apparel manufacturers, beverage manufacturers and distributors, other product manufacturers, and large wholesale distributors. Both parties derive significant benefits from their respective licensing agreements. Manufacturers and large distributors benefit by being able to differentiate their products from others. Sports leagues benefit by "outsourcing." They do not need to create whole new manufacturing divisions that that support the growth of their revenues yet shift their focus away from their core competency. Instead, these organizations use licensing as simply another form of marketing or business development.

You can also structure the licensing or royalty payment your company receives in myriad of ways. Your company can obtain a one-time lump sum up-front payment. Your firm can obtain a small initial payment, followed by additional monthly, quarterly, or annual payments. Or you can make the payments variable instead of fixed and base the payments on a percentage of sales. You must determine the structure that best matches the financing needs of your business, both near-term and long-term.

Attorneys and other agents that specialize in licensing are available. Enlist the services of a highly recommended attorney to help structure the best licensing agreement applicable to your situation, goals, and business model. If you're not sure where to start, check out the newsletters and websites of organizations that cater to industries where licensing is heavily used. These publications often list referrals.

**Pension Funds or 401K.** Individuals can fund the start-up, purchase, or growth of a business venture using retirement funds without incurring penalties for early distribution or taxes. To do this, typically an owner or acquirer of a company creates a C-corporation, then that C-corporation in turn creates a pension plan for the company. The owner then funds the corporation's new retirement plan with all or a portion of his or her own 401K, 403B, IRA or other existing retirement account via a rollover. The new retirement plan subsequently purchases stock in the newly created C-corporation. The funds from the stock purchase are now available as shareholder's equity on the balance sheet to use to grow the business.

Existing businesses can utilize the same process. However, only C corporations can use this method. Therefore, a corporation that files under subchapter S would need to revoke that status. An LLC also would need to convert to a C-corporation to take advantage of this approach to capital.

**Self-directed IRAs.** These have been used for some time by real estate investors as a way to channel their retirement income into real estate purchases. However, these funds can be used to fund or purchase any asset-backed stand-alone entity. The entity MUST be a legally separate business entity –for example, a corporation or an LLC. The deed, debt instrument, loan note, investment agreement, and all other legal documents must be titled to the IRA (i.e., Equity Trust Company, For the Benefit of Joseph Smith IRA), and must be signed by the trustee acting as custodian on behalf of the IRA (i.e., Equity Trust Company).

All funds will go directly from the IRA to the title company, escrow agent, or bank, as directed by the IRA's trustee. The funds can*not* go to the personal account of the person who opened the IRA. Self-directed IRAs can be used to invest in numerous types of special assets including real estate, mortgages, limited liability companies, equipment leasing, and factoring receivables. One limitation: The IRA owner's business may not be located within a property owned by a personal IRA.

**When to use self-directed IRA accounts.** You or a prospective investor have a sizable retirement account but you either cannot take a loan against it (as allowed by many corporate 401K plans) or you do not want to take a loan against it. Neither do you want to liquidate the account and be subject to the penalties for early withdrawal and the tax consequences. The company purchases or develops property for sale or lease or the company uses, sells, or leases other assets.

➨*Example Thirty-Two: A/R, self-directed IRAs, and bank financing.* James started an architectural and engineering firm. He quickly won small government contracts. He obtained a line of credit from an accounts receivable financing firm to cover the expenses associated with fulfilling the contract terms. He was repeatedly turned down for a bank loan with lack of collateral cited as the primary reason.

Mike, a friend of James, recommended that James purchase office space instead of continuing to lease in order to acquire collateral for the company to use in the future. Mike told James about a small office complex at the edge of town, in an area that was rapidly developing. The complex had four separate suites, with only one current vacancy. James could expand into the other offices as the business grew. In the interim, the current tenants would cover the mortgage payments.

James did not have the money for the down payment. He approached Mike for suggestions. Mike said he could use his self-directed IRA to fund $100,000 of the down payment for James. Mike contacted the property's seller and the trustee of his IRA account. The trustee, on Mike's behalf, entered into an agreement with the seller to purchase the property.

Before the transaction closed, Mike drew up a master lease document for James to lease and manage the entire building. The lease included an option to buy which would convert the agreement from a master lease to an installment sale should certain conditions be met. The transaction closed, Mike's IRA trustee's name was placed on the deed, and the master lease went into effect.

One year later, James needed expansion capital. The building had appreciated 25% due to the new real estate developments in the area and improvements he had made. Six months previously, James had triggered the installment sale and now officially owned the building. James approached a bank for a line of credit using the building as collateral. Since the building's loan-to-value now stood at 65% and Mike was able to provide evidence of a good payment history, the bank provided the credit line James needed.

**Swaps or bartering.** This method works well for service providers. Telecommunications firms often swap space on their fiber optic lines. For example, a telecom company with several lines between Chicago and New York would swap space on these lines for space on lines between Dallas and Las Vegas. The space provided would be treated as revenue; the space received would be treated as an expense.

If you are a staffing service company, you can swap providing or screening personnel for a human resource outsourcing firm that will provide you with benefits packaging, payroll and other services. If you are a landscape service company, you can landscape the office grounds of a business consulting firm in exchange for their assistance in addressing the operational and other issues your company may have. These are just a couple of the scenarios available. Bartering opportunities are only limited by your creativity.

If you need ideas, refer to craigslist's bartering section to see what individuals and businesses are currently seeking and offering. You can also barter through business exchanges. You can search for business bartering organizations via Google or Yahoo!

**Utility companies.** Some utility companies will provide project financing for energy or telecommunications intensive projects. If you need to install a huge cooling system for your manufacturing plant, you may be able to convince the local utility company to finance the purchase and installation of this cooling system. The energy company will derive much higher revenues from your company as a result of the installation. Contact the appropriate utility service provider in your area if you are undertaking a worthy project.

**Consignment.** Consignment is when your company takes delivery of an item with a promise to pay a specific amount or percentage of the sales price after your firm sells the product. Consignment works very well for retail stores selling highly differentiated goods, especially apparel, art, or furniture.

**Structured payments.** Companies make structured payments to service providers only after the service provider meets a certain target. These payments typically comprise a percentage of product sales. Companies use structured payments to pay advertising rates, marketing, and sales commissions.

**Service providers funded through grants.** A number of other government grants exist to help companies address specific problems. The Minority Business Development Agency (MBDA) funds Minority Business Enterprise Centers (MBECs) around the country to provide businesses with technical assistance in the following areas: business assessment, strategy, financial packaging, marketing, and operations.

MBECs offer these services as subsidized services. Companies pay according to a sliding scale based on the company's annual revenues.

The SBA funds the Small Business Development Centers (SBDCs) which provide a number of services to and offers training for start-ups, mom and pops and "lifestyle" businesses. The SBA also funds the Service Corp of Retired Executives (SCORE), which provides small business advice and consulting. The Southeastern Trade Adjustment Center (SETAC) provides intensive consulting services to help companies negatively impacted by significant overseas competition move into less competitive industries or compete more effectively in their existing industries.

The Manufacturing Enterprise Program (MEP) is another federally funded program that provides free services to small and medium manufacturing companies. Services include energy assessments, energy adjustments, and lean manufacturing assessments.

## Tax credits.

*Job Training.* Many states and cities fund job training programs offered to lower income residents. To entice employers to hire the programs' graduates, many programs underwrite the cost of the employees for a period of time – typically 30 to 90 days – essentially providing employees free of charge during an initial trial period. Other programs offer tax credits to employers for hiring graduates. Still others provide a hybrid. The purpose of the incentives is to provide low level or minimally experienced individuals with access to jobs that they would have had significant difficulty obtaining on their own. The state or local program does this by paying the wages of these workers for a designated period of time or offering the employer tax credits which cover the employee's wage expense.

*Business or real estate development financing.* The U.S. Congress enacted the Community Renewal Tax Relief Act in 2000 that created the New Markets Tax Credit (NMTC) Program. This program makes investment capital available to businesses in qualifying low-income communities to create jobs and spur additional economic development. The NMTC Program provides tax credits through financial institutions certified as Community Development Entities (CDEs) to companies that locate and operate the bulk of their business in underserved, economically disadvantaged, or blighted areas.

According to the U.S. Treasury Department, "A CDE is a domestic corporation or partnership that is an intermediary vehicle for the provision of loans, investments, or financial counseling in Low-Income Communities. Benefits of being certified as a CDE include being able to apply to receive a New Markets Tax Credit allocation to offer its investors in exchange for equity investments in the CDE and/or its subsidiaries; or to receive loans or investments from other CDEs that have received NMTC allocations."

This program enables taxpayers – individual and corporate – to receive a federal income tax credit in exchange for investing in CDEs which in turn invest in companies that fit specific requirements in terms of location, job creation, and other criteria. More information on the NMTC program is provided at http://www.occ.gov/topics/community-affairs/publications/insights /insights-new-markets-tax-credits.pdf .

For a list of certified CDEs by state, go to http://www.novoco.com/new_markets/resource_files/cde/cde_bystate_080212.pdf. Banks and community investment organizations comprise the majority of CDEs, but participants include private equity firms, SBICs, and microlenders.

Some entities are licensed to dispense the funds in any state nationwide; others can only disburse funds in the states in which they have chartered offices. In conjunction with the location requirements, all require businesses to designate a real estate component as part of their usage of funds in order to access the capital. However, some of the CDEs allow much of the proceeds to fund business development, or operational improvement.

When financial institutions apply for CDE status, they must designate how they will use the proceeds. The awardee designations fall into two categories: real estate financing and business financing. Real estate financing sub-categories include retail, industrial, mixed use, community facilities, office space, and for-sale housing. To determine if your company fits the criteria to access these funds, refer to the websites of the CDEs that serve your state.

In summary, there are many, many sources of cash. It is impossible to cover them all here. The point is to stay flexible, be creative. Speak up. Let people know you are looking for financing. Be careful not to communicate financial duress, but let people know that you seek expansion capital. You may be surprised what people know. People typically only discuss financing options if another person broaches the subject first. When you need help, ask. Research. Read.

**Periodically check out
www.Cash4Impact.com
for updates on more
creative sources of capital.**

PART IV:

# MAKING THE DECISION:
## What is Best for You and Your Business?

# CHAPTER 13

What is best for you?
# Options for non-asset-based small companies

If your venture is a **start-up,** but is not in high technology or manufacturing, follow these steps in the money hunt:

1. *Personal finances.* Tap your checking and savings accounts, mutual funds, and lastly, IRA or other retirement accounts. Get a line of credit on your house or use credit cards. If your start-up is quite small or you have minimal business experience, start the business part-time while still working. Work at it on the weekends and in the evenings. Be cognizant of the business functional areas in which you are weak and seek out training or business classes that will help you address your weaknesses. If your skills are still too weak, begin looking for a business partner. A partner could also contribute start-up funds.

2. ***Friends and family.*** Recruit friends and family as investors or as lenders.

3. ***Banks.*** If you have excellent credit, you may qualify for a small loan for your business that is guaranteed by you. Or you may qualify for a SBA-guaranteed loan, especially if the business has some sort of collateral or if you own your house or other real estate.

4. ***Credit and charge cards.*** Your business banker can provide you with a credit card for your business. You can obtain credit cards from other sources in the name of the business, but guaranteed by you. If you cannot get one in the name of the business, get one in your name and use it ***only*** for the business. Keep good records. Also consider credit cards offered by retailers that provide the supplies you need for your business.

5. ***Microlenders.*** If you do not qualify for bank loans or credit cards, or still need additional funds and your business can pay the debt service, pursue a microloan. The criteria to qualify are more relaxed, and thus, the loans are easier to obtain.

6. ***Swaps or bartering.*** Since you have minimal revenues and income, see if you can swap your services or products or something else you have or have access to with another in lieu of payment. An additional benefit exists for this strategy. When you provide your service and the recipient is happy with your service, you generate a "customer" and word-of-mouth referrals. This "customer" may also later convert to a paying client.

7. ***Factoring.*** As a start-up, unless you have significant contracts, it will be difficult to obtain a line of credit secured by accounts receivables, but you should be able to factor your company's receivables, assuming customers are credit-worthy businesses.

8. ***Equipment financing.*** If your start-up needs equipment, the distributor or manufacturer may provide the financing needed

for you to purchase the equipment. If your credit is spotty, the distributor may still lease you the equipment or lease it to you with the option to buy.

9. *Joint venture.* If you believe you have strong business acumen, a highly desired skill set, or provide a sought-after product or service, then your start-up may be an excellent joint venture partner for the right entity. Do your research to determine what potential competitors or complementary service or product providers would be a good fit and pursue them accordingly.

These are not your only choices, but are *usually* the best ones to pursue if you are in the start-up phase. As a start-up, be wary of undercapitalizing your business or loading up your nascent business with debt. Both scenarios can place your company under undue financial stress and lead to financial failure.

Also, be aware that you need funds not just to *start up* the business. You also need funds to *operate* the business once it is up and running. The money needed to operate the business on a daily, ongoing basis is called working capital. Many companies fail to consider their working capital needs and end up in financial failure.

If your business is a **broker**, follow these steps:

1. *Personal finances.*
2. *Friends and family.*
3. *Factoring and accounts receivable financing.* As a broker in any line of business, your business has minimal, if any, assets. It does not take delivery of any goods, it acts as an intermediary to get the goods or services delivered to the end party. Therefore, your firm often has contracts, purchase orders, or called in orders that convert readily to receivables. These receivables can be used to obtain a line of credit to use

for working capital or can be sold to a factor to obtain the funds to use for working capital.

As a broker, your firm often procures small orders from many different entities. You can use factors to assess the initial creditworthiness of these clients. Once the clients prove that they pay promptly, you can withhold their receivables from the factor going forward. Because of the nature of the business, you should develop a good relationship with a factoring firm even if you only use them to factor and screen brand new clients.

4. ***Banks and direct lenders.*** Typically, unless you own the building your business inhabits and have high margins and ancillary business lines, you are not a good candidate for bank financing. Remember, banks like collateral. Banks will tie up accounts receivables, but do not lend only against receivables. However, you may qualify for an SBA-guaranteed loan because the SBA does allow receivables as the primary loan source for some of its loans. If you have been in business for a few years, have an infrastructure (more than just you the owner and a secretary/receptionist), have increasing margins and revenues, then you are a good candidate for regular SBA loans.

5. ***Microlenders.*** If you are small and need additional capital beyond that provided by accounts receivable financing, then microlenders may be the answer.

Most brokers have operating margins of 3-10%. Because brokering has a very low barrier to entry, the competition for brokers is intense. Therefore, brokers are typically not good candidates for equity financing. If you have a strong infrastructure, operate using standardized systems and procedures, occupy a high margin niche, possess strong customer loyalty, employ five or more employees, and exhibit other characteristics that clearly separate your firm from its competitors, then your business may be a candidate for equity investment.

Read the descriptions and examples to determine what source would likely work best for you and your company.

If your business is a **business services provider**:

1. *Personal finances.*
2. *Friends and family.*
3. *Banks.* Typically, a line of credit is what you will need for your working capital needs. If you are purchasing equipment, computers, and other assets, consider credit cards and trade financing from the seller (store, distributor, or manufacturer). For all other working capital needs – payroll and other payments in advance of payment from customers – a line of credit should suffice.
4. *Credit cards.* Refer to the bank discussion. Use credit cards to purchase office supplies and other materials.
5. *Accounts receivable financing or factoring.* If you have contracts or purchase orders or proposals that you create invoices for, and hence receivables, then accounts receivable financing may work well for you.
6. *Microloans.* If the amount of money you need is low (under $25,000) consider microloans.
7. *Crowdfunding.* If your business sells products or online services that may readily appeal to others, consider crowdfunding. You'll need to create a campaign which includes a video and nice giveaways to attract the most "donators." Shoot for a lower amount, for example $10,000 or $15,000, but continue to pursue funds after you achieve your goal. If you offer products or services that people can order or buy online, then crowdfunding can also help you build your company's customer base.

8. ***Angels***. If you have a rapidly expanding business or have a plan for one, an angel may provide the equity funds you need to grow your business. An angel that is actively involved in the business may also serve as a guarantor for a bank line of credit if your personal credit or your business credit rating is too low to qualify for a loan.

9. ***Equity crowdfunding***. If you do not have any angel candidates in mind or have reached out to some potential angels and not had much success, equity crowdfunding may be a good fit. You will need to have the same types of information that traditional angels want to see, including a good presentation deck. The funders you connect with through equity crowdfunding could provide follow-on financing if they see progress and believe in you and your team.

10. ***Joint venture***.

11. ***Strategic investment***.

12. ***Private equity***. Business service providers such as IT services companies, marketing firms, advertising firms, and business consulting providers (the list goes on) can only attract equity if and when they have a plan to expand regionally or nationally, occupy a strong market niche, or have successfully differentiated their company from their competitors.

    Private equity funds typically need a 20% or greater expected return and – without the larger expansion plans and scope – a business services company will not provide the required returns. You cannot attract equity for your ten- person shop. However, if you have the management team, business development acumen, sales strategy, and operational foundation to grow the business to a 100-person or larger enterprise in a few years, private equity funds may be interested.

13. ***Venture capital***. If your firm provides a business service to which technology is integral to the delivery of the service, venture

capital firms may be interested. IT services firms proliferate, so venture capital funds generally ignore these companies. However, if your company will deliver IT services in a new way using technology, then you may attract the attention of venture capitalists. Venture capitalists may be interested if your firm offers a consulting service which customers can tap into through the Internet, services that your company can monitor through the Internet, or related technology.

Business service firms tend to be small, local operations. Therefore, most firms will not qualify for any equity investment. However, if you want to make the leap from a small consulting type shop with historical revenue of $3 million or less to one with $30 million or more, you need to first create the vision and goals, then the plan to achieve those goals. If necessary, engage business consultants and coaches. They can help you identify the company's and your weak areas and put the things in place to lay the foundation to help you achieve your goals.

If you only reached $3 million in all of the last ten years, and now you want to make the jump to $30 million in five years, you must address the huge credibility gap you are now burdened with. Utilizing consultants and coaches will get you there sooner. These entities can also help you write a plan that incorporates the necessary changes.

If you have been on the path to larger revenue from the beginning, then you do not have the credibility gap with an equity source. However, you must clearly understand and communicate how you are different and how you will achieve revenues of tens of millions when the vast majority of your peers will never come close. This is said not to discourage you, but to simply help you understand what the investors' point of view will be.

If your business is a **professional services (accounting, medical or dental provider, insurance, legal)** firm:

1. ***Personal finances.***
2. ***Friends and family.*** Many professionals tend to be wealthier than those with other careers due to the high incomes many of their professions command. Therefore, similar-minded friends and family often provide a much stronger financial investment base than in other types of businesses. Obviously, your competitors are unlikely to fund you. However, friends in your field in another city or in a different practice area may invest in your business.

   An internist private practice may appeal to a cardiologist. A tax attorney's private practice may appeal to a bankruptcy attorney. A CPA in Atlanta may invest in a CPA's practice in Memphis. Mine your professional associations and network. Many professionals use financial advisors. If you do, ask them for suggestions and solicit them for potential interested parties.
3. ***Banks.*** Banks love professional services firms, especially physicians and dentists. These are often designated as PCs or professional corporations. Why do banks respond so favorably to professional service companies? If the business is unsuccessful (usually due to poor management and operations), the physician can find ready employment as a staff physician at an area hospital and garner a high enough salary to pay back the bank loan out of his or her own income. Similarly, a dentist can join a larger dental organization.

   The same is often true of lawyers who can join large law firms or corporations, and of CPAs who can join large accounting firms or corporations. In most cases, the professional's salary and bonuses covers their living expenses and the debt service on the loans. As a result, the loan failure rate for these loans is much lower than for the general business population making the risk to banks much lower. Hence, the banks look extremely favorably upon these types of business.

4. ***Direct lenders.*** These like professional corporations for the same reasons banks do. If the direct lender finances a lot of professional service companies, such as CIT does for example, then a direct lender may process your loan request and provide you with the funding faster than a bank will. However, it depends on the lender (and the bank).

Generally, professional service firms and professional corporations are not candidates for equity investment except for investments made by the owners and friends and family. These firms tend to be small and highly focused with little growth potential. This very limited growth negates any interest by traditional angels and by any of the other investors higher up the equity food chain.

However, if you are a professional services firm that is building strong, highly standardized operations and systems with the goal of expanding regionally or even nationally, then you fall into a different category. A large, national dentistry provider such as BriteSmile is a great candidate for equity financing. A specialty tax service group like Liberty Tax or Jackson Hewitt or a legal services provider such as PrePaid Legal all qualified for equity financing. If you pursue this route, then nearly all of the equity investment options will be viable options to you at some point in the growth of your company.

## CHAPTER 14

## What is best for you?
# Options for asset-based or rapid growth companies

I f your company is a **non-IT services, high technology** company, follow these steps:

1. *Personal finances.*
2. *Friends and family.* (This source is also called "seed" money.)
3. *SBIR grant.* If you are still in the developmental stage and believe your product can address the needs of one of the federal agencies that fund the SBIR grant, this is a highly viable option for your funding.
4. *Crowdfunding.* If you have a cool product – or can make it seem cool – that is still in development that you can promise to "donors," crowdfunding may be a great option to pursue. The funds can help you finish building out your product and get you through beta stage. And these are funds that you do not

have to pay back in any way, as they are officially considered "donations."

5. **Angel investors.** If you are still in any early stage, i.e., pre-revenue, you will need to engage someone who knows you personally or through a direct referral. Alternatively, you would engage someone who believes strongly in the need for your product or who stands to benefit directly or indirectly from your product. This person will likely want to act in a more hands-on capacity to guide you and your company into the revenue stage successfully. If you have revenues, you can follow the guidelines given in this book for pursuit of angels.

6. **Equity crowdfunding.** If you need several hundred thousand in equity capital and believe your business is at a stage where it will appeal to investors with no personal connection, direct or indirect, to you, then equity crowdfunding will help. Through the appropriate site, you can access potential angel investors much faster than the usual channels when you do not have a network.

7. **Strategic partner or investment.** If an existing company with available cash or credit will benefit from your product, they may consider investing in your company. Build the case, document, and approach them.

8. **Venture capital.** This route is well-known in technology circles and is also covered herein.

9. **Hedge fund IPO.** Refer to PIPE discussion.

10. **Traditional IPO.** Use to obtain the capital to drastically expand your business and to enable your firm's earlier investors, including angels and venture capitalists, to cash out as desired.

Acquisitions by a larger firm are not mentioned because they are a way for the owner and previous investors to cash out, not traditionally a way for a company to obtain expansion capital.

If your company is a **manufacturing company**:

1. ***Before doing anything.*** Think long and hard about actually manufacturing. Is your product special? Are you the only one that can control the manufacturing process properly? Do the margins in your industry provide you with sufficient cash flow and return on your investment? If the answer is yes to all of these questions, proceed.

    If the answer is no, then you should ***strongly*** consider outsourcing the manufacturing to an existing manufacturing company and focusing on the development and marketing of the product. If you need a higher level of security, you can enter into a strategic partnership, joint venture, or focused supplier agreement with the manufacturer(s).

2. ***Personal finances.***

3. ***Friends and family.***

4. ***Bank debt.*** Remember, you may have to shop the deal with a few banks if your own bank turns you down. Focus on the long-term relationship and your growth plans to help you obtain the best loan at the earliest stage. If you do not qualify for the bank's regular loan programs, remember that as a manufacturer you own a lot of assets such as equipment, inventory, real estate, or raw materials. These assets serve as excellent collateral for an SBA-guaranteed loan. Therefore, pursue an SBA-guaranteed loan when you do not meet the regular loan criteria.

    A bank and its banker that focus on serving the needs of its small business clients will often offer the SBA loan as an option if they cannot make the financing work otherwise. However, it is important to be aware of this option in case you are working with bankers that are not flexible or simply are not aware of all their options. (This not infrequently happens when you engage with a bank that does little or no SBA lending.)

5. ***Direct lenders.*** Similar to bank debt but occasionally more flexible, but invariably more expensive.

6. ***Equipment lenders.*** Manufacturing is equipment intensive. If your company does not qualify at this time for bank loans or does not qualify for sufficient bank loans to cover your capital outlays and operating costs, then equipment loans can help bridge the gap. Some equipment manufacturers and distributors may even provide up to 100% financing.

   The likelihood of a higher loan-to-value (LTV) loan increases with the purchase or lease of additional equipment, especially on a staggered time frame. For example, your company buys one large piece of equipment and communicates its intention to purchase another in four months. The equipment provider has four months to observe your company's payment history and build a relationship with you.

7. ***Accounts receivable financing or factoring.*** If your company has contracts or purchase orders with credit-worthy entities and is in a rapid expansion phase, accounts receivable financing is an excellent option. If you must improve your company's financial statements and credit in order to qualify for bank financing, accounts receivable financing is an excellent option. If you cannot obtain the full amount of money you need with the A/R credit line, consider factoring for three to four months while you improve your cash management systems and operating efficiencies. Then switch to an A/R credit line.

   I do not generally recommend using A/R financing continuously for longer than 12-18 months. You must have a plan to move to a cheaper source of financing. However, this financing source is usually a good back-up whenever you encounter significant growth spurts that tax the limits of your existing financing.

8. ***Venture merchant banks.*** These will take a percentage of your company's revenue in exchange for the assistance. However, they can be very helpful in helping you source supply chain relationships and strategically position the company. They want you and your company to succeed so they can get paid.

9. ***Angel investors.*** See prior discussions.

10. ***Hard money.*** Use only as interim financing (also called "bridge" financing) when you are in active discussions with a private equity source or sources but need the capital in the near-term to expand in order to fulfill incoming or imminent orders. If you are expanding in advance of the orders, do ***not*** use hard money if the business does not materialize you will likely encounter difficulty repaying the funds. Hard money should only be used to bridge gaps in funding. You must have a plan or plans to close the gaps. Most hard money loans have a maximum life of three years with 12 – 18 months being the norm and most preferable.

11. ***Private equity investors.*** If you are in a high growth industry, consolidating market, or occupy a strong position in a great niche, private equity firms are interested in you. If they believe your company can generate the returns they seek, they will provide the equity to make the acquisitions or otherwise expand the company. They typically prefer a significant but less than majority stake in the company, usually 30-40%, although it can be as low as 15%.

12. ***Joint ventures.*** Consider joint venturing with a larger manufacturer in your industry or in a complementary industry that wants to make or would consider making inroads into your industry or geographic area.

13. ***Strategic investment.*** Consider an infusion of capital from a key customer or an entity that benefits directly or indirectly from your products.

14. *Hedge funds IPO.* If you have an expansion plan that builds a national or international presence, consider a PIPE, a pursuit of hedge fund investments through an IPO. Enlist the services of a knowledgeable investment banker to assist.

The order of consideration for equity investments will change based on where your company is in its business development activities. If you already use partnerships as part of your general marketing strategy, you would consider tapping these partnerships for equity investments or more formalized joint venture agreements before pursuing outside private equity funds.

Pursuing equity capital from broader sources such as private equity funds requires a significant expenditure of time and effort even when you hire an outside advisor to assist. If you already have candidates, it is far easier to convert those candidates than to "start from scratch" and identify, pursue, and *then* convert the new candidates to actual investors.

If your firm is a **distributor**:

1. *Personal finances.*
2. *Friends and family.*
3. *Banks.* The situation of distributors is similar to that of manufacturers. However, distributors typically own far less equipment and far more inventory. Inventory receives a stronger discount than equipment and, therefore, the collateral requirements may be higher.
4. *Direct lenders.*
5. *Asset-based lenders.* Asset-based lenders such as factors, accounts receivable financing providers, or purchase order finance providers can be an excellent match, if your company has contracts or large purchase orders with credit-worthy entities.
6. *Venture merchant banks.*

7. ***Joint ventures.*** Distributors are excellent candidates for joint ventures with manufacturers wishing to broaden their customer base. Transportation (trucking, shipping) and logistics companies also make excellent joint venture partners since distributors often utilize these entities to ship the goods they distribute.

8. ***Strategic investment.*** For distributors, this is similar to joint ventures. A large current or prospective customer also makes a good strategic investment candidate.

9. ***Private equity funds.*** If you are expanding rapidly into special markets or niches especially those that have been historically underserved or that are growing rapidly, for example, the Hispanic market, your company will appeal to private equity funds. Or if you are consolidating, e.g., growing through acquisitions, your company is an excellent candidate for investment by private equity funds.

10. ***Hedge funds/ IPO.*** If you are a large regional enterprise and have a solid plan to go national, enlist the services of an investment banker to explore the option of tapping into hedge fund investments to fuel your growth. Hedge funds like core businesses with excellent growth potential, as do private equity funds.

If your company is a **transportation company (trucking, shipping, delivery, logistics)**:

1. ***Personal finances.***
2. ***Friends and family.***
3. ***Bank loan or direct lender.***
4. ***Equipment lender.*** You need trucks, lift equipment, and/or storage equipment. Equipment providers are excellent sources for the financing of such equipment. Banks do not typically

finance what they consider "rolling stock" as part of their equipment financing programs.

It is too easy for an owner in default or in danger of defaulting to "roll" the stock to another location to which the bank does not have access, thereby preventing the bank from re-possessing the equipment. The entities that sell, distribute, or manufacture this equipment do not share these concerns as this is the equipment they specialize in. Since they specialize, they know the tricks and the risks, and know how to mitigate them.

5. *Accounts receivable financing or factoring.* If you have receivables, this is a credible financing source.
6. *Venture merchant banks.*
7. *Angel investors.*
8. *Joint ventures.*
9. *Private equity firms.*
10. *Strategic investors.*
11. *Hedge funds/ IPO.*

Transportation companies are often second only to manufacturers in their capital requirements. Due to the high cost of tractor trailers, cabs, load and unload equipment, among others, the capital outlays required to build a transportation company can be substantial.

If your business operates as a **real estate developer or rehabilitator of existing properties**:

1. *Personal finances.*
2. *Friends and family.*
3. *Bank loans.* Many banks provide construction loans to development and rehabilitation projects that the developer draws down as the company completes each phase. Banks can either escrow the funds needed to make the interest payments, capitalize the interest for a period of time, or

provide for monthly interest payments on the construction loans. Interest is typically only paid on those amounts already released (drawn down).

4. ***Self-directed IRAs.*** You can invest your own funds, via the IRA trustee, in any project that does not lease or sale space to your wholly or majority-owned business. Therefore, real estate projects for sale or lease to others qualify. Others can also invest directly in your project through their self-directed IRAs.

   Other investors can either loan funds to the project or invest the funds as equity. For more details, consult with your self-directed IRA's administrator. If you do not have one and want details regarding this option, refer to the information in the section on self-directed IRAs.

5. ***Brokerage accounts.***

6. ***Hard money loans.*** If your company or project does not qualify for a construction or purchase loan from a bank, hard money loans are a good alternative. Several reasons exist for being turned down by a bank. Your credit or your company's credit may be spotty or inadequate or the bank does not lend in the area you target. The quality of the existing structure is too poor or your development resume is too minimal.

   Hard money loans deliver funding within much shorter timeframes than do banks. They also come with the higher likelihood of a fast foreclosure should you exceed the lending term or fail to make the interest payments. Therefore, you must ensure that your project is highly viable. That means you must ensure that you can obtain the permits and approvals needed to begin construction, line up the contractors and subcontractors required to finish construction, and put the agreements and contracts in place that will ensure completion in a timely fashion. I strongly recommend the inclusion of daily penalties to increase the likelihood the contractor finishes on time.

You must create a back-up plan in case you encounter problems with any of the above. You must also ensure that you can lease up and or sell the project or its units in a timely fashion. Line up take-out financing in advance of the project start or shortly after.

If you do all this, hard money loans can be the answer to your prayers.

7. *Joint ventures.* If you are a new developer, pursue another developer with experience to join you in the project. You will likely have to split the project proceeds 50/50 or close to it. Your objective is to learn as much as possible and make money on your first project. If you only intend to do one project, joint venturing may not appeal to you.

However, if you intend to do other projects in the future, the experience, skills, relationships, and contacts the experienced developer brings to the table to help bring the project to fruition will prove invaluable. The benefits of the partner's participation will far surpass the reduction in profits you receive.

If your goal is to be a full-time developer of larger and larger projects in larger and larger geographic areas, you must learn to joint venture successfully. Even multi-billion dollar developers joint venture on some projects, for a variety of reasons. All of the most successful large scale developers have used joint ventures to accelerate their growth. Why should you be any different? You should make it a habit of learning from the best. You are only wise when you learn from the mistakes of others, not just from your own.

In real estate development, some mistakes can be fatal to a project. Use joint ventures to avoid the lethal mistakes and to turbo-charge your development projects. Do not forget, however, to choose wisely. Craft a win-win strategy for both parties in the venture. Then use a business-minded real estate attorney to help you translate that strategy into the appropriate legal documents.

8. ***Private placement (or subscription to limited liability company interests).*** You can set up the project as a limited liability company or limited partnership and sell shares or interests in the project to raise funds. If you do not restrict your pursuit to accredited investors, you must structure your Private Placement Memorandum or Prospectus to clearly state ***all*** of the risks associated with the project.

   You should also state repeatedly that the investor could lose his or her entire investment. If you do ***not*** do this, the LLC or LLP managing partner and you, the primary owner, could be deemed negligent and therefore liable for the monies lost by everyone involved in the deal. Accredited investors are assumed to know this already, but it is still good to clearly delineate the risks, just in case.

Real estate developments do not qualify for most traditional equity investments. Until the developer completes the project, there is no income. Hence, these are not ongoing businesses. The developer pays all proceeds out of sales or leasing up of the units or portions of the project.

However, if you intend to become a real estate development firm and develop properties around the region or nationally, you can raise funds to pursue your development plan. You can form a real estate investment trust (REIT). Once you have a track record or you hire or partner with a firm with a track record, you can create a real estate investment fund to provide the equity needed for the development.

Because real estate provides significant collateral for any lending entity, the huge benefit with real estate is the minimal equity required – in relation to the overall project cost – to build the project or purchase the building.

# CHAPTER 15

# When and How to Seek Outside Assistance

When accessing capital, you may need to enlist the assistance of certain service providers. The specific providers will depend on the amount of capital desired and on the complexity of the transaction. This section provides a description of the advisers that can help you accomplish your objectives in the least possible time in as problem free a manner as possible.

Smaller firms that are pursuing bank loans, microloans, accounts receivable financing and the like may not need to specifically engage one of the advisers described here to assist with the transaction. Many of these capital providers use standard loan documents and agreements to package your financial request. However, you may need help in compiling and presenting the information in the most comprehensive yet succinct format that best meets the need of the entity you are applying to. Why reinvent the wheel? In such cases, the advisers or advising entities described herein can assist you.

**For new or specific service providers, check out www.Cash4Impact.com.**

**Investment banking consultants or advisors.** You can contact an investment bank directly or use an investment banking advisor. An advisor will shop the deal to several investment banks to generate interest and determine who can provide the best and highest amount of financing at the best terms. To evaluate and compare advisors, first consider their track records. What is their record of success? What industries have they served? Next, consider the chemistry. You will be closely aligned with the advisor so you must evaluate the potential for developing a strong and deep trust in these individuals and their capabilities. An adversarial relationship could not only derail the private placement or IPO, but damage one or both of your reputations.

Use an advisor if your CFO does not have experience in transacting mergers and acquisitions or IPOs, as applicable. Also use an advisor if your CFO does not have the time to devote to the very time consuming task of raising money. If you do not have a CFO, find one immediately! You can hire an interim or part-time CFO using a contractual agreement. However you do it, you *need* a CFO when pursuing an IPO, private placement or acquisition.

**Investment bankers.** Some investment banks underwrite, while others do not. The ones who do not underwrite instead partner with larger investment banking firms that do underwrite. As a company matures and grows in size, investment banks become more relevant.

**Attorneys.** Lawyers play an important role in setting up and structuring a new company for rapid expansion. A good transaction attorney is a critical component of a successful business acquisition. Small business owners may need to refer to attorneys for business formation, legal document review (letter of intent, purchase agreement, lease agreements), and employment contracts, among others.

To save money, you can prepare documentation yourself and have an attorney review it or work out a basic fee for service with an individual attorney or small firm. Other options include services such as PrePaid Legal, which now has membership options for the self-employed and businesses with 1-99 employees. An additional option is LegalZoom which provides templates of common types of small business contracts.

Do *not* look in the Yellow Pages for an attorney. Network, get a referral from someone you trust, or contact the American Bar Association. Make sure you state you need a "small business attorney." I was once referred to an attorney who charged $600 per hour for an acquisition. She gave me a quote of $50,000. I later found a mergers and acquisition attorney who only charged me $10,000 for the same outcome.

**Certified Professional Accountants (CPAs).** CPAs are critical to your business. You will enable your business to grow faster to the extent that you utilize a CPA to do more than your annual or quarterly taxes. Knowledgeable, business savvy CPAs understand cash management and asset-based lending in addition to your taxes and can help you navigate pitfalls specific to small businesses and your industry.

**Loan brokers.** When you repeatedly encounter difficulty locating debt financing on your own, contact a loan broker. Get a referral! Many unscrupulous loan brokers exist. These individuals will ask for money up front then never deliver the service they agreed to. If you cannot get a referral, interview two or three brokers *and* interview their references.

The best loan brokers do not charge an up-front fee. They only charge performance fees which they typically structure as a percentage of the financing they obtain for you. That percentage can vary from 1% to 10%, depending on the type of loan and its collateral, the credit rating of the entity or individual behind the entity, and the length of time your business has been in existence. If your loan is fairly straightforward, stick with the brokers whose fees cap at 6%. For more difficult credit and financing situations that require significant effort upon the part of the broker, you should anticipate fees up to 10%.

**Small Business Development Center (SBDC).** These centers, funded by the SBA, provide business plan review and editing and business plan writing classes on an on-going basis. Some centers also provide periodic or annual classroom instruction on financing your business. Most SBDCs provide a free hour of consultation. In addition, many will provide additional technical assistance for growing businesses at an hourly fee generally well below market rate. The SBDC does not typically consider a pure start-up with no revenues, no contracts, and no employees as a growing enterprise. Therefore, most pure start-ups are not eligible for the hourly rate consulting services.

SBDCs operate via grants from the SBA. An organization, typically a nonprofit or university, submits a bid to set up and operate an SBDC. As such, the quality of the counselors provided can range tremendously. Often, a number of SBDCs will reside within one metropolitan area. Therefore, ask around to find what location has the best reputation. In addition, do *not* simply show up at an SBDC office. Call first and make an appointment to meet with a counselor. This increases the probability that you will meet with a counselor who can assist you with your particular business.

**Minority Business Enterprise Center (MBEC) and Native American Business Enterprise Center (NABEC).** These centers, funded by the Minority Business Development Agency (MBDA), provide business assessment, strategy, marketing, financial packaging, operational management consulting and technical assistance to minority-owned companies with revenues of $500,000 and up. The MBDA shifted focus over a decade ago away from "mom and pop" enterprises to larger businesses that are more likely to grow into viable, sustainable enterprises. MBECs and NABECs offer one free hour of consulting to those minority-owned business owners that meet the revenue criteria.

MBECs and NABECs offer the full complement of their services on a sliding scale of $10 to $60 per hour for companies with revenues ranging from under $100,000 ($10 per hour) to $5 million and more ($60 per hour). As with the SBDCs, quality level can vary by center since separate, unrelated entities typically run each center. The MBDA has taken measures to better standardize center performance by raising the base recommended pay of the center consultants and providing training to new consultants through a one week executive training program at Dartmouth's Tuck School of Business.

Note that the operators of the individual centers win a bid process and thus a contract with the MBDA. Consequently, the MBDA does not directly control consultant pay or skill level requirement. Unlike SBDCs, however, typically only one to two centers reside in any one state. Exceptions exist for larger states such as California and Texas.

**Consultants.** Consultants can play a significant role in helping to grow your business to the next level. Consultants can assist with financial packaging, strategic marketing, pinpointing and addressing operational issues. The list goes on. Most small companies eschew the need for consultants. A better way to think of consultants is as another outsourced entity to assist you with what you or another team member cannot do, what you cannot do well, or what you do not have the time to do.

Most small companies do not have the money to hire a full-time CFO. When they do, they most often hire a CPA to do accounting and reporting, neglecting the financial end. Financial consultants or interim CFOs can help bridge the gap – identify and pursue strategic opportunities, align the capital structure accordingly, and obtain the financing needed to achieve overall objectives.

You can find consultants through one of the government-related agencies identified above, through referrals from friends and associates, through LinkedIn and LinkedIn groups, or from your attorney or CPA. As a small business owner, you do *not* want a consultant that specializes in serving corporations. You need someone who has experience working with small businesses and is thus adept at quickly identifying problems, outlining the ways (the plan) to resolve them, then helping to execute the plan. You will have wasted your money if all you end up with is a report even though "the report" is standard consulting modus operandi for many Fortune 1000 companies.

Other individuals and entities that provide general advisory and consulting services to help grow and fund your business include coaches, mentors, trade associations, industry forums, and roundtable groups. The number of coaches has increased significantly. Now several coaching franchises such as The Growth Coach and Action International exist to help you and your company grow. Most coaches are not affiliated with a franchise. If you believe you would benefit from a coach, ask for referrals. Most coaches offer the first coaching session for free providing you with the opportunity to sample before you buy.

To find mentors, tap into your network. Some membership organizations offer mentor services. Approach individuals whom you admire, offer to take them to lunch or dinner then ask them for their ongoing insight. You may have to approach several but, as they say, "Practice makes perfect!" Do not be leery. Many successful people enjoy the opportunity to give back. They take pride in the accomplishments of those they have helped.

Successful roundtable groups, such as Vistage International, bring together a coach or facilitator with a group of business owners from disparate industries. These groups promote a sense of trust. The resulting ability to speak freely enables business owners to tap into the collective wisdom, experience, education, and insight of their peers without fear of competitive leaks or reprisal. Other more loosely formatted groups, such as the Entrepreneur's Organization, offer similar, if less compelling, benefits. However, the price differential is typically significant.

**Business incubators.** One last entity type that does not fit the profile of any specific adviser but, instead provides comprehensive services to its customers, is business incubators. A business incubator is an organization designed to support the success of and increase the survival rate of entrepreneurial companies through the provision of an array of services that may include coaching, networking, physical space, and capital.

Business incubators saw their genesis in the 1970s in response to the ongoing demise of the steel, rubber, automotive, and other manufacturing intensive industries in the Midwest and Northeast. In the 1990s, venture-capital backed incubators sprung up, many of which survived the technology and Internet free fall of 2000 and 2001.

Good business incubators increase the success rate of start-up businesses. According to the National Business Incubation Association (NBIA), (www.nbia.org), 87% of businesses that graduate from incubators are ongoing enterprises that had passed the five year mark. Furthermore, in 2011, incubators assisted 49,000 start-ups employing nearly 200,000 full-time personnel which generated nearly $15 billion in revenue. Communities, institutions, government entities, venture funds, and others support incubators because they consistently produce substantial increases in annual revenues and jobs.

If your company is a start-up or relatively young company, especially in technology, technology-related, or manufacturing, a business incubator may provide you with just the help you need. Good incubators practice selectivity and demand accountability. In return, they often provide increased access to capital through their network. They also provide facilitation, access to resources such as facilities and office equipment, and help with recruiting services on an as-needed, when-needed basis. They also provide non-core resources that enable companies to focus on core business and product development.

Good business incubators provide an additional level of assistance. They provide training, mentoring, and coaching that help you strengthen both your business and your personal business acumen faster. These incubators also reduce the "loneliness" factor, often felt amongst entrepreneurs, most of whom have friends and family who come from employee backgrounds or are still employees.

# About the Author

Tiffany C. Wright is the author of *Solving the Capital Equation: Financing Solutions for Small Businesses* and *Help! I Need Money for My Business Now!* She is the founder and president of The Resourceful CEO (formerly Toca Family Business Services), which provides strategic and financial advisory services, packaged solutions, books, and seminars to small and medium businesses to help owners and managers more effectively manage their companies' operations, finances and cash. Over the last several years, Tiffany has helped companies obtain over $33 million in financing and over $31 million in contracts and purchase orders.

Tiffany leads and coordinates a team of expert consultants focused on working with small to medium businesses. Her expertise is in working with owners and upper level management. Both she and her associates offer management services and advice to clients rethinking the existing financial and operational strategies of their companies. Her extensive problem-solving expertise and knowledge of alternative resources assist companies in finding expedient solutions to specific needs.

Tiffany obtained her BS in Industrial and Systems Engineering from The Ohio State University and her MBA in Finance and Entrepreneurial Management from the University of Pennsylvania's

Wharton School of Business. Tiffany resides in Atlanta, Georgia but can often be seen around her hometown of Akron, Ohio.

Websites: http://**TheResourcefulCEO.com**, www.**Cash4Impact. com** and www.**FinanceYourCompany**.com.

# Resources

The resources provided here, although highly regarded in their respective loan categories, are not meant to be an exhaustive list. Instead, you will benefit most by visiting their websites and learning more about the types of capital they provide and what actions you must take to access it. Determine if this type of financing entity is a good fit for your company. If so, you can then use that knowledge to find companies in your geographic area or industry that can provide similar financing options.

## Accounts Receivable Financing

- **Wells Fargo Capital Finance** – purchased the largest provider of A/R financing in U.S, Commerce Funding, in 2007, folded it into its operations and built this internal group. This division offers several different industry specialties to choose from. https://www.wellsfargo.com/com/financing/capital-finance /accounts-receivable-financing
- **Action Capital Inc.** – operates nationally. In small to medium-sized business market, is second only to Wells Fargo Capital Finance. Has been in existence since 1959. www.actioncapital.com

## Crowdfunding

- **Kickstarter** – currently the largest donation crowdfunding site by dollar volume and number of participants. Has project orientation – films, music, books, and small business projects. www.kickstarter.com
- **Indiegogo** – currently the second largest donation crowdfunding site in the U.S. More focused on non-profits and small businesses. www.indiegogo.com/

## Equipment Loans

- **US Bank Equipment Finance** – one of the largest equipment finance companies in the U.S. Provides equipment and machinery loans from $50,000 to over $50 million. https://www .usbank .com/cgi_w/cfm/commercial_business/products_and_services/ equip_fin_ps.cfm
- **Wells Fargo Equipment Express Loan** – offers flexible loan terms for equipment and vehicle purchases for small businesses up to $100,000. https://www.wellsfargo.com/biz/loans_lines / equipment_express/

## Factoring Firms

- **Eagle Capital Corporation** – somewhat expensive, but highly reputable. Services a large number of transportation-related companies, such as brokers and trucking companies. 1-800-483-7079 or www.eaglecapitalcorp.com
- **Capital Solutions Bancorp** – based in Fort Myers, Florida. Featured in a February 2006 Inc. magazine article. https:// capitalsolutions bancorp.com/
- **CIT Trade Finance** – a subdivision of CIT and one of the largest factoring firms in the U.S. www.cit.com/products-and-services/ trade-finance/factoring-services/index.htm

## Hard Money Financing Firms

- **Kennedy Funding** – finances real estate and related projects. Rates range from 9 to 18% depending on the term and the asset quality (raw land, development project, or purchase). www. kennedyfunding.com
- **Fairview Commercial Lending** – finances residential real estate. Better Business Bureau A+ rating. www.fairviewlending.com/ residential hard money.htm

## Microlenders

- **Accion USA** – one of the largest microlenders in the U.S. Operates nationwide with offices in many major cities throughout the U.S. Loans up to $50,000 for profitable businesses; up to $30,000 for newer, not yet profitable businesses. www.accionusa. org
- **Justine Petersen Housing** – provides small business loans to start-ups and existing businesses in California and Illinois. Also provides technical assistance. www.justinepetersen.org/

## Peer-to-Peer Lending

- **Lending Club** – the largest peer-to-peer lending site by dollar volume. Focuses on high credit worthy companies or guarantors that would often qualify for a bank loan but want more flexibility in the loan terms. The company was founded in 2008. www. lendingclub.com
- **Prosper** – the second largest peer-to-peer lending network. Prosper circumstances "the middleman to connect people who need money with those who have money to invest...so everyone prospers. www.prosper.com
- **WikiLoan** – provides tools that enable friends and family to make loans to one another. Borrowers can access loans from strangers

but on a much more limited basis. Loans range in size from $500 to $25,000. www.wikiloan.com

- **LendingKarma** – different from the previous four loan providers, although it shares many similarities with WikiLoan, LendingKarma does ***not*** provide loans to or from strangers. The company strictly facilitates loans between family members and friends. http://www.lendingkarma.com

## Purchase Order Financing

- **1st Commercial Credit** – provides production finance and Letters of Credit. Targets manufacturers, export and import companies. Operates in the U.S, Canada and the U.K. www.1stcommercialcredit.com /purchase-order-financing/
- **PurchaseOrderFinancing.com** – featured in Entrepreneur magazine and the Washington Post. Will provide up to 100% financing for $500,000 to $25 million in financing needs. www.purchaseorder financing.com

## Venture Merchant Banks

- **Capstone Business Credit** – based in New York City, but operates nationwide. Joseph Ingrassia, managing member. Featured in an Inc. magazine article. 212-755-3636. www.captstonetrade.com/.

Following are some highly respected providers in each equity or hybrid category:

## Angel Networks and Access Points

- **The Atlanta Technology Angels** – http://angelatlanta.com/
- **Network of Business Angels and Investors** – based in Georgia. www.nbai.net/

- **BusinessPartners.com** – similar to Active Capital but the network charges $50 per month to post for angel review. www. businesspartners.com
- **The Capital Network** – www.TheCapitalNetwork.org
- **Startups.co** – www.startups.com
- **Vfinance, Inc.** – www.vfinance.com
- **Cloudstart.com** – this site claims 3,000 accredited investors. Businesses can post for 12 months for $100. www.cloudstart.com / site1.php

## Equity Crowdfunding
- **Circle Up** – established in 2012. Focuses on equity crowdfunding for consumer product companies. http://www. circleup.com/
- **AngelList** – helps connect primarily technology and technology related start-ups with investors, prospective employees and potential partners. www.angel.co

## Incubators
- **ATDC (Atlanta Technology Development Center)** – serves the larger Georgia community. It focuses on early stage technology or biotechnology product and service companies. www.ATDC.org
- **TechStars** – founded in 2007, has expanded to five cities, but remains small to give each company more attention. Helps other incubators. www.TechStars.com
- **LaunchPad LA** – founded in 2009. www.launchpad.la
- **Tech Wildcatters** – based in Dallas, TX. www.TechWildcatters. com
- **Capital Factory** – based in Austin, TX. www.capital factory.com
- **Boom Startup** – based in Salt Lake City, UT. www.boom startup. com
- **AlphaLab** – based in Pittsburgh, PA. www.alphalab.org

## Private Equity Firms
- **Stonehedge Capital** – utilizes state-specific investment funds and tax credits to invest in private companies. Therefore it only funds in states in which it has offices, including Louisiana, Ohio, Florida, and Texas. www.stonehengecapital.com

## Venture Capital Firms
- **Draper Fisher Jurvetson** – based in Menlo Park, CA. www.dfj.com
- **Kleiner Perkins Caufield & Byers** – based in Menlo Park, CA. www.kpcb.com
- **Accel Partners** – based in Palo Alto, CA. www.accel.com
- **CIT GAP Fund** – based in Herndon, VA. www.cit.org/service-lines/cit-gap-funds/
- **Greylock** – based in Waltham, MA. www.greylock.com
- **Trillium Group** – based in Pittsford, NY. www.trillium-group.com
- **Claritas Capital** – based in Nashville, TN. www.claritascapital.com

For a comprehensive list of venture capital firms that are currently funding deals, refer to the National Venture Capital Association. In order to be listed as a member, the venture capital firm must be U.S. based, have a pool of funds of $5 million or higher, and be actively engaged in equity investing. This site also contains information on angel funds and private equity funds. www.nvca.org/index.php?option=com_mtree&Itemid=173

## Mezzanine Financing
- **Small Business Investment Corporations (SBICs)** – www.sbia.org/?page=sbic_program_history

The following are some highly respected providers of non-traditional financing or business support services:

## Self-Directed IRA

- **Equity Trust Company** – visit this company's website for more information on how to use self-directed IRAs to fund investments in real estate or businesses. www.trustetc.com.

## Women-Owned Businesses

- **Women's Business Enterprise National Council (WBENC)** – helps connect successful entrepreneur women with women business owners whose companies are ready to grow. This organization also certifies women-owned businesses. www.wbenc.org

# FREE BONUS RESOURCES

**Get $199 in Bonus Resources for Free!**

This includes the following resources:

- Audio podcasts of the first six chapters
- Sample cash flow worksheet
- Cash flow video explanation
- Video overview of small business financing options
- Video overview of medium business financing options
- Sample Executive Summary
- One-page company profile sheet
- And more

For these free resources and tools, visit:
- www.Cash4 Impact.com/TheFundingIsOutThere/bookextras
- Click *"Access Bonus Resources Now."*
- You will be prompted to enter your name and email address.
- Once entered, click OK and receive your bonus!
- **In addition, the first 100 people to sign up get a free email session (up to 3 email responses tied to the original request) or a 15-minute phone call to discuss their financing needs.**

# Acknowledgments

This book is a compilation of the things I have learned over the past fifteen years since graduating from Wharton. The MBA program at the Wharton School of Business, University of Pennsylvania - through its Entrepreneurial Management major and the business owners and entrepreneurs it brought to campus - first opened my eyes to the myriad ways to finance the purchase or growth of a business. My experience there and in my first post-MBA full time job taught me that there is a solution to any problem – you just have to think creatively. In my job we always found funding, although we often had to change the way we "packaged" our pursuit to match the expectations of those we were pursuing.

I must acknowledge my favorite finance professor, Dr. Franklin Allen, who reinforced my love of my other major, Finance. Another Wharton professor, Professor Ian McMillan, told us that opportunities exist all around us, you just have to learn to see them. I must thank my former mentor, Sharon Goldenberg, a fellow Wharton graduate, and my father for recommending that I document my experiences so I could write a book to help business owners in similar situations.

I must thank all the companies and business owners who I have encountered over the years for continually providing me with the opportunity to learn. I, like most others, learn best by taking written knowledge and applying it.

Thanks to all who helped me put the book together including my former classmate, Hayes Slade, for her insightful critiques and friend, LaShanya Aikerson Sullivan, for her input. I also thank my copy editor, Marc Baldwin's team at Edit911.

Most of all, I'd like to thank my parents. My mom always encouraged me to write and my dad always championed my pursuit of business fundamentals. He also helped review, edit and pre-sell this book.

# INDEX